Creation:
A Scientist's Choice

Zola Levitt

Creation-Life Publishers
San Diego, California 92116

Creation: A Scientist's Choice

First edition copyright © 1976 by SP Publications, Inc. Published by Victor Books, A Division of SP Publications, Wheaton, Illinois.

Second printing: June, 1981
Published by: **Creation-Life Publishers, Inc.**
P. O. Box 15666
San Diego, California 92115

ISBN 0-89051-074-1
Library of Congress Catalog Card No. 76-6781

Printed in the United States of America

Contents

I Was a Secret Evolutionist

Till the day I met Dr. John N. Moore I secretly believed in evolution.

I say "secretly" because Bible-believers aren't supposed to believe in evolution; and I was a certified Bible-believer. Lest the people at church or the readers of my books find out that I was an evolutionist after all, I kept my position secret.

It was almost a secret to me, too, because I couldn't understand my own feelings. I believed in God, but I had not seen Him create the world or its people. I had no objective reason for doubting sincere and intelligent men who held that life had evolved by itself, without help from God.

Then I met Dr. Moore when he was in Texas on a lecture tour. Moore is a professor of natural science at Michigan State University, and I asked him why he, of all people, believed God had created the world. Had he somehow verified this in his laboratory? Had he disproved evolution? Was he a cool-headed scientist or was he a preacher in a white laboratory smock?

I had questions ready for him, and he answered them in a spellbinding, five-hour interview. By the time we parted, he had turned my view of things upside down.

This book is essentially what Dr. Moore related to me that day and amplified during the ensuing months with letters, charts, and scientific verification. This is not strictly a science book, for the material had to be boiled down for a nonscientist to begin with. Nor is it a strictly religious book, for Dr. Moore didn't preach to me.

Instead, this book is sort of a long conversation with an experienced and accomplished scientist who is willing to stand on his beliefs and to present them to those who ask about them.

My belief in the biblical account of creation now rests on solid, objective grounds, and my rejection of evolution as a "theory" * of origins is also unbiased and objective. Anyone may reach the same conclusion, given a chance to listen to Dr. Moore.

ZOLA LEVITT

---

*When reference is made to ideas about first origins, the term *model* is preferable today. Therefore, the word *theory* will appear in quotation marks throughout this book to denote a difference between ideas men have about first origins and well-grounded *scientific* theories, such as the Atomic Theory, the Nuclear Theory, and the Kinetic-Molecular Theory and the Gene Theory.

1
The Difference It Makes

In that first memorable conversation I had with John Moore, we sat facing each other across a table in a hotel conference room. There was nothing on the table—the professor had not brought any charts, notes, or textbooks, to my relief. What he would say was in his head.

He smiled pleasantly and invited my first question.

"Does it really matter to human beings *what* they think about their origin?" I asked. "What difference does it make whether I believe that God created the world or that man evolved?"

His smile grew into the sort of expression a psychiatrist might have when he says to a troubled patient, "I am glad you came to see me because I think I can help you."

"It makes a big difference," he said. "But let's begin with some definitions so we understand what we're talking about."

Three Positions

Dr. Moore went on to say that evolutionists believe that the beginning of life was an accident. Chemicals supposedly combined in a unique way to form a tiny speck of life, which then "evolved" over massive amounts of time into more and more complex organisms. This resulted in the most complex organism to date—man.

Creationists maintain, on the other hand, that God created all matter and life in the forms much as we see them today. Man was made as the creature he is today, in the image of his Maker, and the animals and plants, with all their variety and adaptability, were made by God in successive creative acts (Gen. 1:11-12, 20-27).

Feeling like a sinner making a confession, I told John that my view of things, hazy though it was, allowed for a third position: theistic evolution, a "theory" which states that God did indeed create the world and all life, but He used the slow method of evolution. In my spiritual travels I had come upon this compromise which seemed to merge the Bible and the laboratory.

"Theistic evolution," Dr. Moore said, "is a bad brother of both major models of origins. It satisfies neither the biblical account, which seems to indicate that everything was created in six ordinary days, nor the evolutionary scheme, which needs no God." He went on to point out that Creationists disagree with theistic evolution because it proposes a time-consuming evolutionary process that isn't mentioned in the Scriptures. Theistic evolution also violates the creation principle of each form of life reproducing only "after its kind." Evolutionists disapprove because a creating God is included in a system that needs none; evolution, they assert, happened without a supervising force or a first cause.

A compromise between creation and evolution, Dr. Moore indicated, is unnecessary. The biblical account of creation can be well-grounded scientifically and be used to satisfy all questions, scientific and otherwise.

World Conditions and Evolution

Returning to my original question, John said that it matters profoundly what one believes about the origin of life. "World conditions are a good example of what occurs when people live by evolutionary thinking," he said.

The way we behave toward our fellow man depends on who we think *he* is, and who we think *we* are. If we believe man is a purposeful creation of a loving God, we take a different view of ourselves and others than if we believe we are all evolutionary "accidents." If we believe we are descended from animals, then we will tend to behave like animals, in accordance with such lineage.

John digressed to the virtues of animals, lest I think he, a biologist, did not like animals or their behavior. He said the animals were "good husbanders" and that their behavior was well-ordered and perfectly appropriate to their place in nature. They live by simple rules—might makes right, the fittest survives usually, the superior killer dictates. Animals are regimented into classes based on their relative strength and cunning. Animal societies are extremely materialistic, success being based on the ability to gather food and occupy the more hospitable surroundings peculiar to the particular class. All that makes for efficient, orderly organizations of living creatures which prosper under their systems.

When human beings think of themselves as superior animals, he went on, they tend to live according to animal principles. Animal behavior is not appropriate to human society, John said. Yet, I thought to myself, human totalitarian societies *exaggerate* animal behavior. Animals do not overkill or gather more abundance than they need. They do not seek to dominate territories beyond their own needs, and they do not try to establish control over one another. The more powerful animals do not seek to organize the less powerful into oppressed minorities. Generally, the less powerful are not forced to work for the more powerful. "Live and let live" would more accurately express the animal societies, whereas the dictatorial regimes of men are not above utterly killing out the less powerful.

Human beings do not tolerate well the reign of the "superior killer." The antelope understands that the lion dictates the rules of their relationship, but the antelope does not expect to be tyrannized by another antelope. People are basically like that too, for most human beings have a gut-level distaste for dictatorship and control.

The oppression of peoples—Jews, blacks, kulaks—by other peoples is actually beneath the level of animal behavior. But oppression seems justified by evolutionary thinking, or some derivative of it—these persecuted ones are supposedly not the fittest and so they will not ultimately survive. Killing them out becomes natural.

John gave me his view of the communistic ideology. He believes it originally took off from evolutionary concepts in the age when men learned how to select superior strains of vegetables, swine, cattle, and so forth. Some thinkers, such as Nietzsche, assumed that superior human beings could be selected in the same way.

The selecting of certain plants and animals has been very successful, producing for example, high-quality hybrid corn and leaner swine. The system works well, mainly because people in each area of the world usually agree on what they prefer in the way of vegetables and meat.

What a difference when human beings begin selecting other human beings. Human beings aren't ears of corn or swine (Hitler called "inferior" people *Schwein,* meaning "swine"). And breeding men to produce what somebody considers more desirable traits interferes with human emotion, to say the least.

Evolutionists believe natural selection, the process which tends to cause the perpetuation of desirable genetic qualities and the elimination of undesirable qualities, determines the survival of good corn, and for that matter, human beings. But, men tend to select qualities in domestic organisms according to their own tastes, which is artificial selection. The early evolutionists, Darwin particularly, implied that the selection that occurred in the natural environment could be similar to the selection accomplished by man.

Peoples of different nations struggle. That is "the nature of the beast," we say carelessly. Marx observed this competition among men and assumed that if one class of men could dictate the movements and thoughts of the other classes in their ongoing competition, that controlling class could begin selecting out the fittest men. (Or at least the fittest men in the opinion of that controlling class.)

But this process of central control of human beings by other human beings brought nothing but trouble. We are supposed to get superior men. Instead, we got such men as Hitler and Stalin. Two like them are enough!

Those two set themselves up as selectors of men and they admitted as much. Hitler was especially frank. He said that the Aryan race was superior to all the other races, and especially superior to the Jews.

He conducted breeding experiments with human beings. His *Lebensborn* project, the subject of a 1975 public television documentary, made it a virtue for select unmarried Aryan women to become pregnant by elite Nazi military officers. "Centers of breeding" were set up where men and women were sent to make their contribution to a future superior race. Many of the unfortunate children of these liaisons, the innocent victims of perverted artificial selection, still live and have no illusions of superiority if they are aware of their parentage.

Stalin considered the members of his own political party to be the "fittest" people, and he set about the cruel oppression of hundreds of millions of others. He reigned for an unfortunately long period during which massive numbers of people simply disappeared. Thousands of kulaks, Jews, and other "undesirables" were spirited off to starvation camps and work-to-death prisons in the attempt of one class to dictate to others.

Stalin had no biological excuse for his selecting; his criteria were what men thought rather than how they looked. Those least likely to absorb communism and those who refused to obey its dictates were conveniently wiped out. Somehow Darwin's *The Origin of the Species* led to Solzhenitsyn's *The Gulag Archipelago,* a mind-numbing report of the torture and murder of millions.

Many people are sickened by the tyranny seemingly necessary to the "selection of the fittest." But, the normal aversion of men to these systems may not matter anymore. The reaction may have come too late. At this writing half the world is in the grip of communism, and, in effect, has no opinion.

I began to see, as John went on (and in the ensuing months when I studied his materials and looked into sources of additional information), that it did make a difference whether one held to the creation account of origins or to evolution. Of course, everyone who believes the evolution model isn't a potential Hitler or Stalin, but I did see clearly that totalitarian regimes, with their ruling "selectors," did seem to have roots in the evolutionary way of thinking. And if one believes that men are evolved animals, responsible to no Creator, subject to "improvement" by artificial selection, it is only a short step to believing that pure materialism and selective breeding would be good for the human race.

I told John that I agreed that totalitarian systems were bad, but I pointed out that most of the free world does not subscribe to such excesses.

"Well, evolution is being taught in our schools," he answered.

I hadn't thought much about it. I was taught evolution as a fact when I went to school, and no alternative was presented.

Charts in our schoolbooks showed the classification into various species and their presumed relationship to one another. I had always assumed that I was studying established scientific fact.

Dr. Moore conceded that the plant and animal genetics I had studied were probably valid, but that the classifications were purely arbitrary. The scenarios of man's past—those series of pictures representing a succession of apes growing ever more man-like—were just that: scenarios. The complex interrelationships of fossils were all arbitrary. Even the dates were speculative; nobody really knew how old the fossils were, and apparently they were given very early dates to allow time for evolution. What I studied were the unproved "theories" of men, not scientific facts. Studying "theories" was OK, but no one had *told* me they were "theories."

It is unfortunate, Dr. Moore said, that school children are taught evolution as if it were fact. Attached to scientific fact is a respect for it, or at least behavior to conform to it. Each child, apprehending the idea of the survival of the fittest, wishes naturally to become the fittest. It's not that they become bestial, but they begin to compete with one another in the cold and unforgiving manner of animal competition. Animal competition is influenced by restraining rules of instinct and proportion, but the creative human being can be a more cunning competitor. By the time children become teenagers, they have had a prolonged exposure to evolution and the implications of it. They begin to see themselves and others as evolved animals rather than the creations of a caring Creator.

Finally, the finished adult emerges as a fierce competitor, covetous and materialistic.

Of course, the sin nature of man—his natural propensity to acquisitiveness and selfishness—operates, but evolutionary thinking hardly relaxes the tendency. In the manner that evolutionary philosophy gave Hitler and Stalin *excuses* for their systems, the idea that men are improved animals gives materialistic people an excuse for excess.

It's hardly fair to the animals. As Will Rogers once said, "I like a dog. He never does anything political."

World Conditions and Creation

I asked John how people came out when they believed the biblical account rather than evolution. If it made a difference what a person believed about origins, those believing creation ought to come out a lot different than those believing evolution.

John said they did. Where creation is believed there is an entirely different social result. Not that people carry out the letter of the Scriptures; I'd known enough Christians to know that they vary in their faith a great deal. But something happens inside the people that makes them give the Gospel a real try. And that makes all the difference in the world.

"Believing in creation requires, of course, belief in God, the Creator, and in the order of creation set forth in His Word," John began.

With creation there is no substance to the concept of "the fittest." There are no valid criteria for selecting one man, or a class of men, over another. God created the first man as able and fit as men are today (even better—sinless to begin with—but that's another story).

True, God chose a man, Abraham, and a nation, Israel, to accomplish His special purposes, but there are two vital differences between these selections by God and the selections attempted by men. First, the Selector in this case is the Creator, and therefore a perfect selector by definition. Second, Abraham was not chosen for his particular mission because he was more fit in some natural way than other men. We see no indication in Scripture (Gen. 12; Deut. 7:6-8) that Abraham was physically superior to other men. In fact, many believe that God's point in choosing Abraham was to demonstrate that *any* man, however fit or unfit, may accomplish a great deal by following the will of God. The life lived by Abraham and the long history of Israel seem to demonstrate that each prospered or failed according to how he followed God, not through any human superiority or special effort on his part.

Since men have not evolved into anything superior over the time since creation, there is no point to the struggle over "survival of the fittest." Everyone survives according to God's plan for him as an individual. Satan's classic line, "God helps him who helps himself," loses all meaning—man was created with all the needed capabilities to begin with, and does not require further help, at least in a worldly way.

Under the creation system we find that man was given dominion over a created world. This emphasizes not only respect for one's fellow man—also a caretaker of the world—but over nature as well. Pollution, over-utilization of natural resources, over-population which can cause famine—these become very serious concerns to those entrusted with dominion over the world. Under the evolution system man's excesses and the ruination of the world are just other phenomena of his animal inclinations. Under creation these matters become serious moral concerns.

If people were to take God's view of themselves and others, Dr. Moore said, love and trust would become characteristic of the peoples of the world. Selection systems of men and women, with their accompanying inequities, would be unthinkable in that kind of society. Persecution of any human beings would be repugnant to those imbued with the respect for individuality and freedom inherent in created beings.

The creation system also has a future, in that God's Word accounts for not only the beginning of the system but the end as well. Where the future of evolution is hazy (is some superior kind of creature going to replace us?), the prophecy in the Bible is most explicit about where we are going. A downward plunge is expected, toward a coming period of tribulation in the Bible. The ancient Hebrew prophets and the Book of Revelation agree in forecasting an extremely materialistic and totalitarian regime in the "end times," and many Bible students feel that this is almost upon us.

Trusting in the total creation system, which includes the salvation of believing men, will make a big difference. According to the Scriptures, those men believing in God, obtaining their salvation through the sacrifice of Christ, have eternal life and will survive the most heinous of worldly regimes. Men differ on the timing and fulfillments of prophecy, but the promise of eternal life to believers is most clear in the Scriptures.

Obviously, death has a big impact on the evolutionist. Death ends his sojourn on earth, which looks all the more brief considering that vast amounts of time passed before him. The pointlessness of accidental life becomes confounding to the materialistic evolutionist at the point of his death. His tiny spark is snuffed out, with no reason ever having been announced for its existence, and no reason for its demise.

The believer in God, the Creator, and His Son and co-Creator,

Jesus Christ, goes on, however. His Creator remembers him and as surely as he was created for a purpose to begin with, he is appointed to go on with his Creator eternally.

A "philosophy" such as eternal life has no place in evolution, where only the fittest live beyond the normal lifetime. But, the concept of eternal life is surely the greatest difference between the two systems, and it surely has the greatest impact on the individual. Whether we are to live or die is a question everyone is interested in, even if he wears a white lab coat. We surely live differently when we believe that what we do will have an everlasting impact on others.

Then, if everyone were to take creation seriously—creation and the rest of the Bible, including the Gospel—this might be quite a different world. Our country has experienced a kind of long-term creation-evolution experiment, and unfortunately the trend seems to be going toward evolution.

Dr. Moore briefly sketched the American spiritual history, starting with the fact that this nation was first settled by Christians who sought freedom of worship. "This country was very Bible-oriented in its first hundred years or so," he said, "and most of our great universities started out as church schools. We used to teach creation as the basis of origins." But more recently, he went on, America has changed to an evolution orientation and this has been accompanied by a marked departure from our former high moral and ethical standards.

In effect, when we used to respect the Scriptures and practice the admonitions of our Creator this was a better nation. A large portion of the Scriptures is devoted to the up-and-down affairs of another nation—Israel—in respect to how they adhered to Scripture. We may be failing to grasp that lesson.

John wrapped up his talk on the differences between believing evolution and believing creation on that point. His view of the world, and particularly this nation, is not unlike his view of the laboratory; he watches what happens and he draws conclusions.

At this point in our talks, I began to see that the belief in creation was preferable. But could I believe in it just because it was preferable?

I was eager to get this scientist into his own familiar territory, scientific fact, and understand why, from his informed position, creation was the better alternative. My attitude was one of excitement, I should say, because this man seemed to know what he was talking about.

I wanted to stop being a closet evolutionist, and I could already see my closet door opening and a little light coming in.

2

The Evolution Trip

Dr. Moore's explanation of evolution was the best science, the best history, and the best religion I'd heard for a long time. I wanted to hear more. I will summarize what he told me.

A Clue to Natural History

Evolution is an attractive idea—a way of explaining a lot of mysteries about the world. There is a pretty fair philosophical case for it, and it fits nicely many ways men like to think. It's materialistic, simple, and, at least on the surface, orderly. Evolution seems to answer a lot of questions. And frankly, evolution relieves men of a lot of moral responsibility.

Man arrived at evolution in an attempt to explain his world and his past. By observing the world as it is, man has been able to come up with ingenious reconstructions of what might have gone on before.

The physical world offers many clues to the past, and the geological scientists have assembled an impressive amount of data and have formulated many interesting interpretations of what may have transpired. Rock strata indicate that the earth has undergone geologic changes. Earthquakes occur regularly, so they must have always happened, and they made big changes. Volcanic eruptions and the presence of deep valleys—the V-shaped ones supposedly

17

cut by streams and the U-shaped ones by glaciers—are interpreted as evidence of great environmental changes. We know that bodies of water were distributed differently in the past; what is now a desert was once covered with water.

A natural, reasonable assumption is that living things must have also undergone dramatic changes as the earth changed. Many fossils—impressions or remains of plants and animals—have been found in rocks; some of the fossils indicate creatures now extinct. Other creatures, whom evolutionists thought had been extinct for millions of years, have been found to still exist. One example is the coelacanth, a lobe-finned fish which was found near South Africa in 1938.

Seeing the present animal life of the earth, men got the idea of families of various species. There are similarities between different kinds of creatures—fish and reptiles, monkeys and man. Careful studies of the animals reveal remarkable likenesses in the internal body systems, the embryos, and the skeletons. The apparent interrelationship of the internal systems of animals and man seems to justify the relationships of observed outward characteristics.

Well-preserved skeletons have been found, but they look like pre-creatures of animals which exist now. The skulls of mammoths, gigantic animals now extinct, resemble elephant skulls. Even skulls of past apes look like skulls of present men, according to some evolutionists; and other skeletal parts have been interpreted as man-like forms. Other scientists interpret the same skeletal remains as evidence of degenerate, inbred people who lived several millennia ago, but were contemporary with the most ancient human beings on record.

So man reasons that some creatures made it to the present day and some didn't. He then notes that certain variations of characteristics can be produced by selective breeding. He breeds plants to obtain certain characteristics, like the hybrid sweet corn. He places his superior animals together to produce following generations of still more superior animals.

And man notes from these experiments that the beneficial characteristics in a species can be made to survive. He reasons that beneficial characteristics might have been caused by chance in nature to produce the surviving creatures we have on the earth today. The better hunter in the forest lived to produce more offspring. The offspring inherited the advantageous characteristics of the better hunter, and so it went.

In the science laboratory the remarkable tendency of organisms to establish more virile strains was observed under controlled conditions. Certain strains of bacteria and flies appeared which were resistant to the penicillin and DDT that were lethal to the original generations. The "fittest" were surviving.

The survival of the fittest creatures is a phenomenon observed in the animal kingdom where the stronger and better prevail. It seems intellectually palatable to assume that the "fittest" creature of all—man—came from the fittest creatures among the animals.

This involves quite a strange idea—one kind of creature changing into another, though no one has ever seen one kind evolve from another kind. But, to the evolutionist, the idea is good for a number of reasons. It explains the extinction of some animals. It agrees with what has been observed in animal life—that the more able creature prospers. And it pretty well gets rid of the idea of a Creator who planned all this.

The History of Evolutionary "Theory"

Though Darwin did not conceive the idea of evolution, he made it generally acceptable with his *The Origin of Species,* which was first published in 1859. His logic appealed to the young scientists, and in time evolution had the charisma of a religious doctrine—its early adherents were called converts.

The newly popular "theory" of evolution dovetailed with an advancing secularism. People were beginning to believe the higher critics, who attacked the inerrancy of the Bible. Darwin's explanation of the mysteries of origin was most satifying to people looking for freedom from religious dogma.

Men had tried to explain the world in materialistic terms since before the days of the ancient Greek philosophers. Hundreds of years later, in the seventeenth and eighteenth centuries, adherence to Christianity declined in scholarly circles as men placed more and more confidence in the sciences. In this "age of enlightenment," new discoveries in chemistry and physics, the industrial revolution, new levels of public health and comfort all promised a new world in which reason could explain everything.

In this atmosphere many men, such as Lamarck and Diderot,

whose writings were influential, accepted unquestioningly the view of man as an improving animal. Everyone wanted to fit everything into the clever "theory" of evolution, which Darwin made appropriately palatable. Progress seemed inevitable.

Evolution gradually replaced creation, first in the universities and then in the secondary and elementary schools.

The famous Scopes trial in 1925 focused public attention on the battle between evolution and creation in a court of law. The outcome was inconclusive, but science teachers increasingly accepted the "theory."

Somewhere along the way evolution, still unobserved, and therefore not scientifically determined, seemed to take on all the characteristics of observed and repeatable scientific fact. It "fit in" so well with established scientific theories that it was gradually thought of as one of them, without the normal birthright.

Today, most American scientists believe the "theory" and accept it as if it were proved. They teach it in the universities, giving it the same credence as any proved fact of any science. Because of its charisma and general acceptance, the professors *assume* it to be true.

But the best explanation for the acceptance of evolution is that it satisfies mankind's tendency toward spiritual unbelief.

The Bible clearly states that no man seeks after God (Rom. 3:11) but even without scriptural corroboration it is obvious. Men do not want to believe in God, so they seek for systems that disallow Him.

In modern times the conflict between creation and evolution is very clear. It seems that what is of faith is not of science. (Yet, science definitely involves faith in basic presuppositions.)

Scientists have made great strides in the past century, but so have religious scholars, in the sense of verification of the Bible, revival among learned men, and worldwide evangelism. But comparatively few scientists give credence to anything religious.

Yet, there is no need for this historical divergence between the disciplines to continue. Scientific activity does not preclude God. Rather, in the view of believing scientists, true science is a means to discovery of more of God's creation. Biblical references to scientific principles are being understood for the first time today, and a construction of first origins based on the creation model has not been ruled out by any scientific discovery.

Science and theology should be merged as they once were (theology was once called "the queen of sciences"). With scientists unveiling the picture of man's material life and theologians enlightening man's spiritual side, the quality of man's progress would be much improved. As it is, religion without the Bible, and science without true faith have led man into a desperate situation. We are about to destroy the whole world with our scientific know-how while masses of our race deny that man *has* a spiritual nature.

Evolution also prospers today because of man's general moral state. Man has been a sinner since the Garden, but today wars move us closer to nuclear destruction, tyranny threatens the human rights of millions, and immorality, promoted through improved mass media, is heard about and copied much faster than ever before. A purely materialistic way of thinking about things—such as evolution provides—is soothing to the human conscience. If we are only animals, then it must be OK for us to behave like animals, or at least animal behavior can be expected. There is no such thing as sin, because *sin* implies transgression of absolute laws defined by a Supreme Being who is absolute good. Many of the laws of our land are based on God's law as given in the Scriptures. But breaking the law as defined by our courts and breaking the law defined by God are quite different things. One has only to notice the numerous actions and attitudes condemned in God's Word but which are legal in man's governments to realize that man does not have a clear idea of what sin is. Adultery, for example, clearly sin in the Scriptures, is not condemned by law in most societies. Nor are hatred, pride, and envy.

People tend to live by their own laws rather than by God's, and thus are more comfortable with evolution than creation. Give us our evolutionary status and we think we're free to sin without being punished. But make us God's creations and we have God to answer to.

This brings up the biblical teaching about the devil. Satan is well aware of creation and its implications for men. The men who believe in creation realize they have a responsibility to a Creator and they are less likely to follow Satan's recommendations. They look to a kingdom beyond this world and tend to guide themselves toward it accordingly.

But, for the majority of human beings, evolution is a masterpiece. Satan has contrived to satisfy man's natural curiosity about his nature and his world with a "theory" that excludes the Creator and seems to answer all questions, or at least all superficial questions. The "theory" fulfills a great desire—the desire to do as one pleases.

Reflections of a Closet Evolutionist

I had never thought of evolution as "a way of explaining things," but as the truth about things. I had certainly never thought scientists could have biases or be prey to "pop theories."

As a former college student and university teacher, I know how quickly "theories" become dogma in the world of education, how sacred the "theories" of the "learned ones" are held to be. I could see how evolution caused a stir, became accepted by a few worthies, and then rapidly became the fashionable way of thinking about our origins.

But on the other hand, I thought, John presented a pretty fair case for evolution. He had not presented scientific data hard to refute, but as he described the "theory" and its background I began to want to believe it again. It seemed simpler, it seemed the way to go. After all, I was one of those school kids who came sometime after Darwin; I had a secret respect for these ideas, and for what my own teachers had regarded as truth.

I knew Dr. Moore was in no way for evolution; he had described it in unbiased terms, calling evolution a "theory." He had qualified many of his statements with "seemed to suggest," giving me the feeling that he would be adept at knocking down the "theory." But I was beginning to wonder.

I hoped that when I asked him why he did *not* go along with evolution he would have clear evidence. I hoped he could raise solid doubts in my mind about evolution.

I wanted to end up in the position of someone who had never read the Bible but was still able to resist evolution simply because it was not fact.

I challenged him to make me doubt evolution.

3
Facts about a "Theory"

A Conversation

Dr. Moore: "Science can be divided into two main kinds of activities—empirical and theoretical. The first deals with things that can be observed, like rain, cows, gas consumption, and measles. The second has to do with things that can't be observed, like atoms, genes, the future, and the past."

Mr. Levitt: "Wait a second. Don't scientists work with atoms and genes all the time? And don't they work on the future and the past too?"

Dr. Moore: "Yes, but in different ways than they work with the things they can see and touch. Atomic research depends on the theoretical side of science. Much of what is known about atoms is reliable—earlier theories have been verified and new techniques of "seeing" atomic activity tend to support the assumptions about the atom. But nobody has ever seen one, yet.

"Certain experiments have been successfully repeated at will, and the existence of atoms and genes is now taken for granted. But that is not the case with the past, and certainly not the case with evolution.

"You just have to be very careful with something so 'theoretical' as an idea about first origins. You cannot directly test the past. What you have to do is choose a 'theory' and test it *indirectly*.

23

You can make predictions from your 'theory' of the past and see if they work out. But there's no such thing as observing the past.

"Now I think I can show you two important issues about evolution that will cause you to doubt it. First, I can show you that it is purely 'theoretical,' even speculative—it is not based on observable events. It consists of assumptions primarily. And second, what we know about the earth and life on the earth—what is truly observable today—fails to show evolution of one kind from another kind.

"In short, I think I can show you that evolution is only an opinion and that it has no support."

Mr. Levitt: "If you can show me that, I'll doubt it."

Similarities and Variations

The history of science is replete with discarded theories, each of which was once a good idea. Men once thought that the earth was flat; we have observed that this is not true. Men also thought that living things arose spontaneously from non-living material. We have now observed that this is not true.

Examining the data of the case for evolution, we can find a great deal of it highly suspicious. Most "historical" geology, such as the movements of continental glaciers and formation of valleys, is unscientific in that no human being can report on the way great valleys were formed or the way continental glaciers actually moved. There is no repeatable observation to depend on. Scientifically, we don't know how rocks of any kind and shape are formed, except for certain examples of volcanic rocks.

True, we have clues, or at least we can observe what geological formations we now have and postulate where they came from. But this is not to be confused with scientific study. Formulations about geological phenomena may appear quite reasonable but still remain untested.

The fossils, too, are all dead and we have only their present appearance to observe. This does not conclusively demonstrate anything about their lineage. A fossil may be similar to a living organism, but this is inconclusive. I may resemble a portrait of my friend's grandfather, but that does not make me his descendant. My son may resemble a college student at another university, but that does not make the stranger a relative of my son.

Historical variations on the earth's surface do indicate past environmental changes, of course, but these seem to point more to catastrophic changes rather than the leisurely changes associated with so-called geological evolution. In any case, the idea remains totally unobserved.

Animal similarities are a fascinating area of study and used to give a great deal of credence to evolution. "Ladders of animal life" have been constructed to show an orderly progression from the single-celled creatures to the more complex creatures, with man at the top of the ladder.

But the evolution of similar external characteristics, skeletons, embryos, and blood, rests on the assumption *that the degree of similarity between two animals describes their degree of relationship.* Thereby man is more likely related to the ape than to the frog, and more likely related to the frog than to the earthworm.

This assumption, reasonable as it sounds, has no scientific basis. Many exceptions to it crop up. The myna bird and the parrot excel at mimicking human speech, an outstanding human characteristic, but this does not make them our relatives.

Assumptions, it should be said, have their proper place in scientific investigation. An assumption based on available evidence gives a starting point for testing. Hypotheses are constructed as the beginning of scientific experimentation.

But, of course, hypotheses (as answers to problems) only gain validity as they pass the rigorous tests of observation and replicability. We must be able to demonstrate the truth of our hypothesis to the satisfaction of an observer, and to be able to repeat the demonstration. What we would have otherwise might be reasonable and persuasive, but it would not be scientifically valid.

Assumptions can be tricky. Let me give you an example from within the "theory" of evolution, concerning mutations among the living things. Earlier we mentioned the strains of DDT-resistant flies and penicillin-resistant bacteria. Under laboratory conditions they seemed to have established more virile strains which were resistant to drugs that originally were lethal to them.

So it appears to the evolutionist that the bacteria and the flies developed new strains which have the resistance capacity, and that this demonstrates evolution in progress, with the new generations superior to the old.

But this reasoning, based on the *assumption* that mutations can produce new traits, states that a certain strain of bacteria, confronted with penicillin, develops through the generations resistance to the penicillin.

Without evaluating that, let's choose a different assumption. Let's assume that some bacteria were unaffected by penicillin in the first place. We didn't know, after all, what effect penicillin had on bacteria until we used it.

Under this new assumption we observe that the unaffected bacteria go on reproducing while the affected ones are killed out by the penicillin. This will simply create a bacteria community with a much higher proportion of the unaffected strain.

Under our second assumption it would be quite incorrect to assume that our new community was a matter of superior creatures that had evolved from inferior ones. It would be correct to say only that the original unaffected ones are still unaffected and now make up a greater proportion of the total community than before.

We can see immediately that an assumption has a great deal to do with the conclusion reached, and in true scientific investigation such biases must always be identified.

To date, scientists have not shown that mutations result in new traits in any living organism. It has been observed that mutations only modify existing traits. Thus, the assumption of the first case given above—that the bacteria evolved into something new and superior—is unfounded in science. Our second assumption agrees with existing data and explains the phenomenon of the penicillin-resistant bacteria.

In spite of that, evolutionists insist on seeing mutations as the raw material upon which natural selection acts. There is no scientific basis for this.

The popular idea of survival of the fittest as an evolutionary process ranks with "historical" geology as a "proof." It has not been observed, nor is it scientifically observable today.

We might conclude that the most superior animal of them all is the infamous sacred cow which survives anything.

Evolutionists offer the many variations among the living organisms as support for their "theory," but essentially they offer no more variations within a group. One may arrange the monkeys in a ladder based on what we understand of their traits, but the ladder merely shows differences between family members. To add man at the top of the ladder and describe an orderly hierarchy is not scientifically valid. No genetic relationship between monkeys and man is known.

It challenges many evolutionists to learn that Darwin's *Origin of the Species,* the bible of evolutionary thinking, contains only evidences of variations *within* organism groups. There is no case given of one animal group evolving into another.

An example of Darwin's evidences are the celebrated finches of the Galapagos Islands, which show remarkable variations in size of bills, feeding habits, perching habits, coloration and other characteristics. These birds display many differences of appearance and behavior as do human beings, but like human beings they are all of the same kind. They are truly a highly varied species.

But they are still all finches.

No doubt Darwin did not intend to found a school on materialistic philosophy when he stated his views on the variations of organisms. As an imaginative observer of nature, he advanced an intriguing series of speculations on origin of species. Though initially rather religious, Darwin gradually lost confidence in the Bible and doubted it as a form of revelation. He drifted toward unbelief, stopping short of claiming atheism, but he never returned to faith in God as some have erroneously claimed. How his ideas have been used by those who followed him is very intriguing.

The social or intellectual acceptance of evolution is simply not a matter of accurate judgment of scientific data. It *is* in keeping with the times, with the materialistic view of things, and with the virtual worship of science, a latter-day phenomenon. But broad acceptance does not make evolution scientifically valid.

It is almost as if members of the scientific community *want* to trust an unproved "theory." Instead of accepting that animals vary greatly within kinds, a scientifically observable phenomenon that answers all cases, they want to believe a "liberating" idea which does away with a Creator. Through evolution they can supposedly break away from the "chains of the ignorant past," to reach new stages of advancement.

The scientific community may be overstraining itself to justify the adoration of the past century. In this scientific age, no thinking person questions the value and validity of scientific progress. But people have been asking nagging questions of scientists: Where did we come from? Why are we here? How did the world get here? Many scientists are persuaded that evolution gives them some answers to offer.

Of course the answers aren't really satisfying. If we "came from" a lesser animal down the line, our ancestors must have originally come from a single cell of life. But evolutionists have no explanation for the origin of that cell. To say that it was formed by the accidental combination of certain chemicals is to beg the question of where the chemicals came from. If the chemicals came floating out of the universe, we must ask where the universe came from.

The "theory" of evolution only raises new questions, and makes evolution a matter of faith rather than a method of true scientific investigation.

Now for some hard data about life and the earth which fail to support the "theory" of evolution.

Genetics

Evolutionists believe that all life resulted from a single cell and that along the way different combinations of organisms appeared. That is, mutations occurred as the generations progressed, and over a supposed long period of time, beneficial mutations tended to bring forth more complex and superior organisms. As these recombined with each other, presumable beneficial mutations became emphasized, and finally we had extremely sophisticated creatures.

There are many problems with that reasoning—and it is only reasoning, since there is no evidence of it whatever. What is *known* about mutations is that they do not result in new *traits* in any organism. Also far from advancing a species, most genetic mutations are harmful to the species. Mutations among human beings are a simple example—we call them "birth *defects*" for good reason.

Since mutations produce only variations in organisms, it is difficult to see whole new species resulting from mutations. And as most mutations are harmful to the progress of a given species, it is difficult to see how improvement to so-called higher creatures might have occurred.

Now, variations in organisms are observed to occur only within kinds. Darwin's finches, you remember, were highly varied, but still finches. Evolutionists argue that variation represents some kind of progression, ultimately leading to another species, but this is simply not part of scientific data.

Whenever we attempt to connect one kind to another by mutation or variation, we invariably end up with "breeding gaps." The incipient organisms—the ones that supposedly bridge the gap between one kind and another—are not there. If there is any sort of progression between one species and another, no one has seen it or produced any evidence of it.

It is significant that without success genetics has been tried and tried in an effort to produce some evidence of evolution. If an experimenter causes an organism to vary, whether it be plant or animal, he always ends with what he started. If he starts with bacteria he ends with bacteria. If he starts with moths he ends with moths. He may cause all sorts of differences within that kind of organism by the introduction of chemicals and so forth, but he always finds that he is limited to the plant or animal he works with. He often gets a somewhat poorer variation of his species.

So, the area of genetics and variations has not produced evidence of evolution.

Classification

The classifications of plants and animals, charted in almost every high school biology textbook, are arbitrary groupings of organisms based on the degree of similarity observed. Reptiles and fish bear a greater similarity than do birds and apes, for example, so we tend to group reptiles and fish together. But now comes the assumption; we look at the classifications and tend to assume that similar creatures are related in some way. The evolutionist goes a step further and assumes that similar creatures have a common ancestor—reptiles and fish are similar because they "evolved" along the same line of mutations from some ancestral creature's in the past. A "gene pool" is imagined from which supposedly came creatures that appear similar. A whole history of increasingly more complex creatures is supposed, and a classification chart is drawn.

The facts in the area of classification also argue against evolution. We observe no connection between distinct groups of organisms. Living things bear a sharply defined fixity of kinds. Clear differences between basic characteristics of different groups always remain, suggesting that they do not have a common source at all. These basic characteristics persist regardless of how much we may try to vary them. It appears instead that the various groups, either plants or animals, have been discrete, or unrelated, from their very beginnings. There is no evidence of any sort of common history of distinct groups.

The "gene pool" idea and the "pedigree" charts men make from it have no basis in fact.

Looking further into the similarity of organisms, we do find similar skeletal structures and similar embryoes among the creatures we tend to classify together. Fish and reptiles do have these things in common, to some degree, as do monkeys and humans, to some degree. But we must be careful about supposing a high degree of relationship just because of a similarity. Working with the highly similar organisms, we have still found no connection between kinds; fish are still fish and reptiles still reptiles. We have found no evidence of a common ancestor or gene pool being responsible for similar skeletal or embryonic characteristics.

Fossils

Fossils represent a fairly reliable look into the past. Going along with evolution, for the moment, we would expect to find out missing creatures to fill our "breeding gaps." There should be a geological record extending from the assumed gene pool, through all of the variations, to the complex creatures we have now. We might not expect to find every single step on the ladder of life, but we ought to find at least an orderly progression.

We've found nothing like that at all.

We've found large numbers of fossils of all sorts, but these have not closed the gaps. We have found no complete "geological column," or layer-by-layer fossils showing an orderly succession of life forms. It is often *said* that the geological column is there, and it is even *taught* that it is there, but it simply has not turned up. The incipient creatures—those intermediate forms of organisms—are completely missing. Often the layers of fossils we have found do not appear in the proper evolutionary order.

We simply find fossils in the "wrong" places—fossils of marine animals have been found on mountaintops. The locations of the fossils are wrong only in the sense that they fail to demonstrate evolution, the original assumption of some men about our history.

The Genesis flood, if I may mention it, would account for the misplacement of the fossils.

It is interesting that we have found fossils of animal kinds that exist today; that is, we may come across a fossil of a gopher which is essentially the same as the gopher we now have. Because of these "living fossils," we may argue strongly for fixity of kinds rather than for evolution. Our gopher, one case among many, seems to have missed out on evolution.

Dr. Henry Morris, of the Institute for Creation Research, San Diego, Cal., remains unchallenged in his direct statement, "The fossil record, which supposedly documents the history of life on earth, contains no incipient or transitional kinds between major categories of biological organisms, exactly as predicted by the creation model but contrary to the hopes and expectations of evolutionists" (*Introducing Scientific Creation into the Public Schools,* Institute for Creation Research, 1975).

Furthermore, when we talk about fossils, or most any issue out of the past, we must always consider the accuracy of our estimates of dating. Evolutionists suppose that the earth is millions, billions, or even an infinite number of years old, and this is convenient to the proponents of the "theory" of evolution. Evolution requires a great deal of time, given the leisureliness of the supposed geological changes, the mutations, and the long history needed since the initial gene pool. It is almost taken for granted among evolutionists that adequate time has elapsed for all these processes to take place.

But again we run into difficulties. Evidences are found of a "young" earth, with certain fossils of complex organisms buried entirely too deeply. Nickel and other elements in the ocean, helium in the atmosphere, are not abundant enough to have been present for millions of years—hence, the earth could be very young. Rocks turn up consistently in "wrong ages." The chance combinations required for the presumed evolution of living organisms by mutation and variation could only occur over enormous amounts of time—and that much time is simply not available according to present knowledge.

The dating of the earth and of various fossils and rocks rests on very shaky ground, and many scientists, even of the evolutionary persuasion, agree that the time-measurement devices need more examination. The different methods used—radiometric, nonradiometric, the geological column—all hazard certain assumptions. Chemical methods depend on the assumption that certain chemicals have always decayed at a constant rate, have never become contaminated, and have always acted in the manner they do in present-day experiments. Geological methods, as we have seen, depend on accepting the idea that evolution has taken place and that we can expect to find older, less complex creatures in lower layers of the "geological column."

Dating is not a scientific process, given the limits of our knowledge at present. We have no way of observing how much or how little time passed before us. From fossils and rocks we may interpret *what* existed before us, but in no clear way can men tell *when* those things existed.

The Scientific Study of First Origins

It is supposed that as we gain knowledge evolution will be verified. It's assumed that we simply haven't yet found out what we need to know to prove this attractive idea, but verification is just around the corner. Evolutionists have faith in their "theory." That's why they call what appear to be nonexistent organisms, such as the incipient fossils, "missing"—missing links.

DNA, the basic molecule of life, was supposed to provide proof of evolution. DNA research and protein analysis is a rather recent area of inquiry and at first it looked as if the research pointed to a basic principle of evolution—that all organisms were made of the same building blocks. It also appeared that the DNA molecule was identical throughout the animal kingdom.

But the breakthrough didn't work out. As biochemists became more able to identify explicitly the protein nature of tissue in various living organisms, the highly distinctive qualities of the DNA molecule became apparent. What has emerged seems to illustrate what the Apostle Paul pointed out—there is a fundamental difference in the flesh of men, of fishes, of beasts, and of fowl (1 Cor. 15:39). We do know as fact that the DNA molecule varies with the species.

This particular research is germane because it is right up to date. It comes, as it were, after a century of unsuccessful efforts to prove evolution. But it amounts to the most potent proof we have of *discreteness*, not relationship, of the species.

But in what seems to be a die-hard effort, evolutionists have placed the new protein data on the old classification charts. They found the DNA *similar* in the various species and they again assumed relationship of the species. So now we find the DNA listed along with the similarities of skeletal structure, embryos, and all the rest, as another "evidence" of the evolution of the species.

It's the same old difficulty—the initial assumption seems to dictate the interpretation of findings. Once they start along the evolution road, they try to fit everything in that comes along.

There is no repeatable experiment that verifies the supposed connection between kinds due to the DNA similarity. It's the same story that it was with the mutations, the variations, the skeletons, the embryos, and on and on. No experiment has been done, no evidence produced, no scientific conclusion reached on any genetic connection between basic kinds. The evolutionists have at best proved again what they proved before—that organisms are similar but discrete. Similarity has not, thus far, proved relationship. There is variability of life but always within basic stability of kinds of living organisms.

It has been widely supposed by the nonscientists that work going on in laboratories turns up evidence of evolution. This is not true now, and it has never been true. When all is said and done—when the experimenter has finished causing variations in his bacteria and moths—he ends up proving that the discreteness of the kinds is inviolable.

The big problem confronting the evolutionist lies with his heavy burden of assumptions. The initial assumption—that life has evolved—has become especially burdensome as our knowledge has progressed. At this point it seems obvious that the data we have about life cannot be used to support an evolutionary past. If we just leave the assumptions alone and look at what we really have before us—the discreteness of the kinds, the absence of "intermediate" creatures, the lack of observable evidence of the past—we cannot arrive at evolution.

Reflections of a Closet Evolutionist

I had not realized what was *not* going on in the scientific laboratories. I had thought, probably like most nonscientists, that evolution had been scientifically established, or was on the verge of being scientifically established. This was evidently *not* the case.

But I was determined to remain a skeptic. A doubt about my own possible biases crept into the back of my mind. So, I wanted Dr. Moore to talk to me about creation in the same way as he talked to me about evolution, as another "theory" of origins.

Dr. Moore and I had to part company at this point in our discussions because his tour in Texas was finished. He promised to carry on the discussion by letter and by phone, and to address himself to creation in the same manner as he did to evolution.

4

The Creation Trip

I thought the whole matter of creation was quite simple—one believes in God, and then he takes on faith that God made everything. But Dr. Moore meant to cover all sides of this issue. What follows is the essence of his correspondence.

Theistic Evolution

Theistic evolution, a "theory" which states that God created the world by using the evolutionary process, seems to be a "bad brother" of both evolution and creation—an attempt to reconcile ideas that just can't be put together. It would be simple if God were an evolutionist after all, and created the world and all life according to what scientists say they are discovering in the area of evolution. But theistic evolutionists, in accepting the many precepts of evolution, violate the biblical account of our origins in many essentials.

Evolution involves an entirely different order of appearance of the animals and plants than is given in Genesis. The idea that all varieties of life spring from one-celled creatures rests, in turn, on the idea that life appeared in the order of increasing complexity; whereas, according to Genesis *all* manner of life appeared at God's word on the third, fifth, and sixth days of creation (1:11, 20-21, 24-26). Also, according to theistic evolution, all the creatures could be interrelated, but their definite discreteness is described in Genesis. That all creatures reproduce only after their own kinds is stressed in the Genesis account.

Finally, there is the time factor. Theistic evolutionists must accept the eons of time necessary for evolution while rejecting the Bible history of the earth which fits into only a few thousand years at most. Evolutionists of all stripes opt for millions, billions, and beyond.

Materialistic evolutionists object to theistic evolution very strongly because they don't see the need of God at all. The point is that evolutionists posit a purely mechanistic explanation of the earth and of life. The entrance of God into their system is clumsy and extraneous; they think their system works fine without Him.

Some scientific-minded people who are religious in the sense that they believe in God would like to see a reconciliation between God and science. Theistic evolution appears to fill this need, but the "theory" seems unnecessary. We have seen that God has no real quibble with true science, or vice versa. We might better try to reconcile *the data we have* with the Genesis account. This data gives a very reasonable case for creation.

An alternate system of origins which violates any of the elements of the creation model would not be biblical creation. Hence theistic evolution is in sharp disagreement with the biblical account.

How do we go about believing in creation? Do we all have to be Ph.D.s to be able to appreciate the biology, geology, and chemisty of this complex world? No. A layman's observation of the world around him, combined with the keys to understanding it provided in the Scriptures, gives a satisfactory picture of our origins.

God, Kinds, and the Flood

The existence of God, the Creator, is, of course, the most important element in the creation model, and the data we have to observe is the earth and the life on it. We cannot see God and we have not seen Him create the world. Our data, in this case, is limited to what we now have around us, and what has been preserved from the past.

Complexity clearly suggests an intelligent Originator. If the astronauts, while walking on the moon, had come upon a wrist-watch lying in the dust, they would have assumed that men had been there before them, or that some intelligent, wristwatch-making creatures lived on the moon. Their very last assumption would have been that the materials on the moon had somehow combined spontaneously to make a wristwatch.

The earthly "wristwatch," the incredibly complex interrelationships of environments and intricately formed creatures, must have come from a "Master Plan" or at least from a purposeful Designer.

In an effort to account for a purposeful Creator, some men have proposed that life on the earth was placed here by superior creatures from somewhere else. We are but a shadowbox display or a lab experiment for some highly advanced creatures in outer space. But this idea fails to account for the origin of such superior experimenters. A satisfactory "theory" of origins must account for *all* origins.

Likewise, the idea of the accidental formation of original life forms from randomly floating chemicals is not an answer to the question of the origin of the chemicals. Who made *them?*

However we style our purposeful creation scenarios, we are invariably brought back to a single Creator who always existed.

The second element of the creation model is fixity of kinds. We can observe that the life of the earth reproduces only after their kinds, as we find in the Genesis account (1:11—2:27). We have no evidence that one kind of creature evolves into another but we have a wealth of evidence that each creature reproduces its own kind. When we plant tomato seeds we expect to get tomatoes. We *see* that human beings come from human beings, but monkeys come from monkeys. We have no *evidence* of man coming from monkeys, or any other such relationship of the kinds of animals. When we looked at genetics, we saw that the *data we have* agrees with the fixity of kinds principle. We saw also that we might *suppose* some kind of relationship of the kinds because of similarities in skeletons, embryos, and general appearance, but this supposition involved an extra assumption about our data. If we make *no* assumptions about our data, sticking to *what we see,* we have the fixity of kinds principle steadily demonstrated.

For the Flood (Gen. 7:10—8:3), the third element of the creation model, we have no such observable evidence. Here we must examine the earth's crust and the fossils of animals and plants to see if there are traces of this past catastrophic event. Admittedly, this kind of evidence isn't as strong as the evidence for the fixity of kinds, which is demonstrated steadily in the present world.

Our data includes the observable present world, and we find an interesting distribution of the rocks of the world which suggest the Flood. The most commonly found rocks throughout the world are sedimentary rocks, which were laid down under water according to geologists. Debris from eroded rocks and particles from weathering of rocks were transported from higher places to lower places via running water. Few contend with this reasonable interpretation. Because of the generous and apparently random distribution of these rocks, creationists believe tremendous volumes of water at some time in the past were present throughout the world.

Furthermore, the sedimentary rocks are relatively soft and are good "recorders" of past animal and plant life. Fossils are abundant in sedimentary rocks. But, interestingly, the fossils also seem to be randomly distributed, and many are found in surprising locations. Marine animal fossils appear far from the sea, for example, in landlocked areas or even on mountaintops, as mentioned earlier. Was this due to a mighty movement of the rocks or the animals at some past time through a catastrophic, not slow, event? The fossil record is often buried in the "wrong" order of life, as we said earlier and, regarding the Flood, creationists interpret the masses of fossils as the result of a sudden burial by catastrophic means.

Mountain ranges and canyons on the ocean floor could be due to worldwide movements of the earth's crust at some past time. If the irregularities in the crust of the earth were made by a great force at some past moment, the Flood would be a good possibility.

Fossil, or polystrate, tree trunks are found in many places on the earth. They are completely surrounded by hardened rock debris in many layers of sedimentary rock. How such polystrate fossils came to be is a real mystery to evolutionary geologists. The Flood would account for these trees, and many scientists, not necessarily of the creationist persuasion, assume local past flooding. One worldwide flood would be a simpler explanation than many local floods imagined by evolutionists.

Again, we are looking at evidences out of the past, and we

are reconstructing what seems likely to have happened. But, the evidences of the rocks, the fossils, the crust of the earth, the trees and much more data, seem to support the possibility of a world-wide catastrophic flood. No other interpretation is any stronger. Several fascinating books for the layman treat the Flood question in its entirety (e.g., *The Genesis Flood* by John C. Whitcomb and Henry Morris, and *The Earth That Perished* by John C. Whitcomb).

The Decline of This World

The creation model also deals with the future. Surprisingly good scientific testimony supports the biblical prediction of a coming major change in the earth and in the life of the earth. The psalmist wrote: "Of old thou didst found the earth; and the heavens are the work of Thy hands. Even they will perish . . . and all of them will wear out like a garment, like clothing Thou wilt change them, and they will be changed" (Ps. 102:25-27, NASB). The Apostle John saw in his revelation "a new heaven and a new earth, for the first heaven and the first earth were passed away" (Rev. 21:1-2).

This agrees remarkably with a tested scientific law—the second law of thermodynamics. According to this law, the available amount of energy in a closed system continually decreases. Life systems on earth, all dependent on solar energy, must eventually die. There is, of course, no observer of these future events, but the decline of energy from the sun is a scientific fact.

We are also seeing a decline in genetics. The "genetic load," the collected characteristics of living things, is a manifestation of deterioration—especially in human beings. More and more undesirable gene mutations seem to be occurring, or at least we are becoming more and more aware of a significant genetic load of deleterious gene material in living things. This is not to be expected according to the mechanical system of evolution, in which an improvement of life is anticipated. The impressive gains we ought to be seeing in a system where life is constantly improving are just not there.

Thus, the biblical predictions of the future seem more realistic than the predictions of evolutionary scientists. We cannot prove the coming change, but we can scientifically show the decline of the present system, and that this decline is to be expected according to the creation model.

Time and Creation

There is the problem of time in the creation system. The Bible begins with the words "In the beginning God . . ." and seems to give an unbroken line of history of ten thousand years at most. Creationists posit a "young earth." God may have created an earth with the appearance of age, but He created it relatively recently. But, people have become convinced that the earth is very old, and that all life came into being very slowly. It *is* *difficult* to imagine that our complex environment and the life we see around us were created in six days. And the few thousand years suggested in the Bible don't seem enough for the history of the whole earth and for the history of man.

On the other hand, if we accept the existence of an almighty God, how fast He can do His work becomes a moot question.

Observable data in this are slim, admittedly, but we *can* question the necessity of the millions or billions of years posited by evolutionists. These extreme amounts of time have been built up in order that evolution might seem possible in the first place. Without the evolution concept we have no reason to suppose a lengthy history.

The time estimation devices now utilized by scientists are suspect, as we saw when we talked about evolution. The chemicals that are present with us now do undergo changes over periods of time, but we have no way of knowing if they behaved this way in the past, and we do not know what their condition was at "the beginning." In fact, we have no "zero-setting" for our "historical clocks" at all.

In any case, the problem is greatly simplified when we consider the intriguing idea that God could have created an "aged" earth— an earth with the *appearance* of age. Evidently, according to the Scriptures, God created the first man and woman as adults, and they were surrounded by mature animals and vegetation. Logically extending this phenomenon to the earth, God may have created it in a mature state, complete with mountains and valleys. When Jesus made wine (John 2), He accomplished in a moment what is normally a time-consuming process. We must consider that God, if we accept His existence at all, has the ability to do quickly what we ourselves consider very lengthy processes.

By now we have discovered that there is something more to the creation model of origins than pure faith. Nevertheless, faith is a vital part of this model, as we noted before about the evolution model, and without faith we cannot appreciate the validity of the model at all. Therefore, our discussion must move to how belief works in both science and religion.

Reflections of a Closet Evolutionist

I looked forward to John's next discussion. "Hearing" an experienced scientist express himself on faith and how it works "in both science and religion" was going to be a rare event for me. I had always assumed that faith and science were mutually exclusive.

Before Dr. Moore's discussion on creation, I had not realized all that there is to creation. Believing in God, for me, had been different from believing in the Flood, the fixity of kinds among the animals, the future mentioned in the Bible, and the "young earth" we live on. These things seemed more like matters to be decided by the local church or by some board of experts. But the presence of God in all these things can almost be felt.

Dr. Moore made one thing crystal clear: Creation is given in the Scriptures, or we're talking about some other model of origins. The Flood, to John, is an issue for objective discussion. He expects to find evidence of it in the geology and fossils of the world, and he has no doubts that it was a real event. His belief in the Flood is part of this total reliance on Scripture. The Flood was a real event, at least where John is concerned about explaining the creation model, and is part of his total reliance on the Scriptures.

Prophecy, to John Moore, is an objective matter, or at least he looks at the conclusions of prophecy objectively. The second law of thermodynamics and the Book of Revelation seemed unrelated to me before my encounter with this unique scientist, but now I could see the connection.

The questions remaining in my mind had to do with the areas where John had admitted lack of evidence. After all, how could we convince anybody of an area where we didn't have all the data? How was our case for creation better than the evolutionist's case for his "theory" if both simply depend on faith? Was our faith "better" or more reasonable than the faith of the evolutionists?

I needed what Dr. Moore was coming to—a discussion of faith and how it works.

5
A Rationale
for Belief

While I waited for John's letter about faith, I went to a copy of another letter on the same subject. This letter was addressed to my people—it's called the Book of Hebrews—and it contained just the matter I had been searching for: "Faith is . . . the evidence of things unseen" (Heb. 11:1).

The writer, well-educated, competent to discuss subtle issues with the philosophy-loving Greeks of his time, took up the matter of faith in great detail, and he related it to man's history in Hebrews 11. Then, as now, people were wondering about the things they could not see. Unobservable data was to the writer and everyone else a matter of great importance. Regarding God, he wrote, "Without faith it is impossible to please Him" (11:6).

The author of this epistle pointed out that Noah had great faith and that it worked to his advantage when the flood came: "By faith Noah, being warned of God of things not seen as yet, moved with fear (reverence), prepared an ark to the saving of his house" (11:7). Other New Testament writers and the Lord Himself often referred to the biblical events which are a part of the creation model.

Creation and Faith
But faith in God is an old story; and I expected to find many ref-

erences to it in God's Word. The faith that I was becoming interested in was the faith in science, or at least in those parts of science which are more or less accepted but are not proved. When one is "scientific" these days, one is modern and objective. "Scientific" things have a certain charisma. TV commercials repeat again and again the latest "scientific" tests and surveys to establish the superiority of nearly every item on the market.

The phenomenon of the virtual deification of science is profitable for the image-makers, since scientists, to give them their due, have contributed much to modern life. People appreciate that scientists, who have been able to conquer dread diseases, also place men on the moon and construct horrifyingly potent weapons of global war, have a profound effect on life. The image-makers have simply built upon an established potent image.

But it is a mistake to credit scientists with more than they know. The scientist worthy of the calling sets out to add information to the collected body of scientific truth, not to sully that truth with undue suppositions and assumptions. The true scientist does not wish his hypotheses to be regarded as fact.

Newspaper columnist Dr. John F. Anderson, Jr., pointed out many of the problems with what he calls "Scientism"—the religion of science. He described the modern-day, worldwide "enchantment with technology" in connection with the Apollo-Soyuz space flight. I quote in part Dr. Anderson's very applicable column:

> So many startling developments have emerged from the laboratory in this century that many rush on to the conclusion that "science is the funeral director who has buried ancient, outmoded Christianity in the cemetery of human error." Some act as if a new religion has emerged. Scientism is its name, the Ph.D. is its high priest, and the appliance service is its deacon.
>
> After all, is not a person's religion revealed by what he or she worships, by what is believed to be the very core support of life itself? Cannot all questions, they argue, be answered ultimately by scientific research? Is not this the road to the solution to all human problems—hunger, poverty, disease, ignorance, limitations of space—and even, perhaps, death itself?
>
> This is not a tirade against science, but rather a protest against scientism considered to be the only discipline worthy of human attention.

One mistake of scientism is its claim that faith is unnecessary. Actually, the physical scientist is forced to use faith of a sort. An integral part of the "scientific method" is the hypothesis, i.e., "proceeding as if something is true."

That happens to be as good a definition of faith as can be found. Moreover, the very assumption that reality can always be measured, that nothing exists which cannot be seen, felt, tasted or touched is a daring leap of faith.

Science does have its place—to answer the question, "How?" But that is not enough; we also need to know why and wherefore. We are much closer to the truth when we find a faith adequate to interpret our observable facts and give them meaning.

Scientific inquiry can be a religious activity in that it can be one mode of God's revelation. Every experience and experiment is an encounter with reality—some reality to which we can give no other name than God. No wonder the psalmist exclaimed, "The heavens are telling the glory of God; and the firmament proclaims His handiwork " (Psalm 19:1).

A complete knowledge of all matter and of all interacting energy forces is not enough. The scientist also needs a faith to motivate, to control, to enable him to address the Ultimate Reality with a prayer such as that of Angela Morgan:

> "Dear Lord, I am aware of a splendor that ties
> All the things of the earth to the things of the skies;
> Here in my body the heavenly heat,
> Here in my flesh the melodious beat
> Of the planets that circle Divinity's feet." *

If the scientist needs "a faith to motivate, to control, to enable him to address the Ultimate Reality . . ." as Dr. Anderson asserts, then the creationist certainly does too. Dr. Moore had helped me approach the creation model scientifically, carefully separating observable data from conjecture, and our activities had led to the area of faith. We came to a point where the evidence ended.

At least we were willing to call faith, faith. But I still wondered

*John F. Anderson, Jr., "Down to Earth: 'Scientism' Not Complete Answer." Reprinted with permission.

how the case for creation was better than the case for evolution if both finally came down to a matter of faith. Dr. Moore had indicated that creation is somehow a more rational object of faith than the other model. The case he presented drew me out of my closet.

A Case for Creation

The philosophical case for creation takes in the broad cause-and-effect relationship and uniformity of events that are vital to all investigative intellectual activity. Here again, by observation of proved data, we come to a very good case for creation.

The scientist assumes a regularity of naturally occurring events, and he sets out to study those events in his particular specialty. He assumes that he will be able to find pattern or order, which is required in scientific inquiry. He believes that he will be able to identify regularities which he can then formalize into generalizations, and even into laws, from which he will be able to make reliable predictions about all similar events.

The scientist is always looking for reliable cause-and-effect relationships in the world. He *assumes* that some cause, or causes, is involved in bringing about a certain effect he has observed. This "faith" approach has been most successful in the work of the physical scientists, and most biological scientists want to take the same direction.

But study of the biological science fields is greatly influenced by the peculiar area of evolutionary thinking, by which scientists posit non-factual suppositions first and then try to assign observed data to them. The cause-and-effect principle, so reliable in other fields of inquiry, seems to be laid aside in favor of a "theory" which intrigues.

The creationist wishes to follow the established cause-and-effect procedure without recourse to any particular "theory" other than Scripture. And then the idea is to objectively compare known data with the biblical revelations.

Scripture differs from the evolution model in that it does not describe a system with missing parts yet to be found. As we have seen, it presents all relevant data in orderly fashion, and can be more readily verified in many details.

For example, the creationist begins with the known fact that human beings come from other human beings. This is quite differ-

ent from the supposition that man first came from some other organisms, though it is observable that human beings come from
human beings. The creationist then progresses to the next question
—where did the first woman come from?

Right at that juncture the creationist and evolutionist part
company. The creationist realizes that *no scientific* observable
answer can ever be found about the origin of the first woman, so
he answers the question biblically, saying that the first woman came
from the first man, who had been created by an act of God. A
human being came from a human being (see Gen. 2). The creationist takes this answer as his beginning point, as a "given."
Then the creationist examines observable data and finds that
human beings come from human beings. Therefore the creationist
assumes that human beings have always come from human beings
since the first pair come into existence.

The evolutionist, on the other hand, departs from known data
and posits another unobservable system. Conjecture and speculation come into the "scientific" picture as the evolutionist thinks
about "what might have happened" under certain conditions that
might have occurred sometime in the distant past. This is known
as the "probabilistic" position. Evolution-minded scientists are
prone to talk about the probabilities of things occurring rather
than sticking closely to known cause-and-effect relationships.

Biologists have probably been encouraged to think in probabilities because of the success of scientific research into subatomic
particles which has involved the relativistic, probabilistic thinking
of Einstein. This research has led to solid, repeatable, and
statistically sound research. But biologists have invented hypotheses about origins which are almost wild in nature.

Like the ancient Greeks, who enjoyed ceaselessly debating issues but were disinclined toward directly studying the issues,
the early evolutionists began to hypothesize creatively. The well-
known "probable," "could," "might," crept into scientific textbooks as the boundaries of reasonable speculation were steadily
extended. Finally, a family of evolutionary scientists came into
being: evolutionary biologists, astronomers, biochemists, and
"historical" geologists. (Within the field of geology, the dichotomy
between those working with proved data and those working with
"scenarios" is clearly seen. The highly reliable research of the
physical geologists, prospecting for mineral resources and pe-

troleum, stands in sharp contrast to the fruitless labors of the "historical" geologists, hunting for a hypothetical past.)

So both the creationist and the evolutionist make an assumption about the First Cause—the cause that started everything—the creationist believing in an eternal God, and the evolutionist in eternal matter.

Evolutionists and many other people are inclined to snub the God-idea because creationists assume a Creator without a beginning, which is how God is described in the Bible. Most people don't stop to think that evolutionists also assume a "creator" without a beginning in positing that matter somehow combined to form life. This matter has no beginning in the evolution model and must have existed before anything else. When the evolutionist says, "This combined with that," it can always be asked, "Where did 'this' and 'that' come from?"

Finally, both faiths depend on the possibilities of examining those first causes. Have we any way of verifying God? Have we any way of verifying eternally existing matter?

We have at least a written record of the God-idea. We haven't the slightest evidence of eternally existing matter, and the mind balks at the very idea. The Bible can be read, analyzed, compared with history, archaelogy, and geology, to evaluate it for reliability. The other model, evolution, is without empirical evidence and must be taken purely on faith.

The reliability of the Bible is a special study, but let us briefly show that archaelogical researchers invariably verify the Bible. Some of the most suspect passages of historical or geographical Scripture have been proved by scientific investigation. For example, the family names of Genesis 10 have been found, in identical or markedly similar form, in the ancient tells or mounds that archaelogists are now uncovering.

For some time, skeptics contended that the Pentateuch, the first five books of the Bible, could not have been written down by Moses or anyone else of his time because the art of writing hadn't yet been developed. It was once held by historians and Bible critics that writing was not developed till the time of King David, about 1000 B.C. But, now we have written documents, signed by their authors, from the fourth dynasty of Egypt, predating Moses. We know, in fact, that Moses had a choice of languages. He might have written in Egyptian hieroglyphics, studied as he was in Egyptian tradition, in Akkadian, which was extant, or in ancient Hebrew.

The existence of Abraham was also in question for quite some time before archaeologists unearthed cities mentioned in connection with him, evidences of the very battles he fought, and documents containing place and personality names in Abraham's life. If Abraham were mythical, it has been generally conceded, definitive evidences which support the biblical record about him would not likely be found. Ur, Abraham's birthplace, was once thought to be mythical, but it has now been unearthed to reveal tombs, houses, schools, and libraries, still in good condition.

Archaeologists have dealt likewise with the biblical record of the destruction of Solomon's Temple in Jerusalem, the existence of the Hittite people, and the very wording of the books of the Bible. The Dead Sea Scrolls, a most exciting find in modern Israel, verify the ancient reportage to a degree that utterly discounts the idea of mythology. No archaeologists thus far have uncovered anything really out of place or time as given in the Scriptures.

Prophecy is similar to another kind of evidence accepted in the most critical scientific circles, that is, support of predictions from a basic set of assumptions is an accepted way of testing those assumptions. The Bible authors "assumed" a great deal about the future. The recovery of Israel in modern times and the animosity of Russia toward that state are just a few of the many fulfillments of biblical prophecies hazarded thousands of years ago (Russia—"Magog" in Ezek. 38—39).

The best that can be said to those who doubt the scriptural accounts is that the accounts sometimes seem doubtful. But, as they are verified, it becomes more reasonable that they truly are accounts of actual events. Thus the creationist is utilizing as source material a type of multiple observations, much as modern scientists do when they rely on test and re-test of their hypotheses in the laboratories.

Reasonable Faith

Faith in the Bible, therefore, is not so unreasonable a faith as some critics would assume. Apart from our fascination with this ancient best-seller, the evidence continues to accumulate that it is as accurate as the authors say that it is.

This is an important point in considering the case for creation. Faith is a part of *every* kind of human belief, whether one believes in science, religion, politics, or anything else. The question to be settled is how rational a particular faith is in respect to observable data. Should archaeologists find even one important artifact out of place or out of the time sequence reported in the Scriptures, the entire Bible becomes somewhat suspect. Our faith in it ought to decrease with such a find if we are being reasonable. But conversely, as the finds confirm the Bible, our faith in its reportage grows.

Likewise in science, the faith a true scientist has in a particular model must necessarily be connected with the available evidence supporting or denying that model. We have a very high degree of faith in physical geology as specialists find mineral and petroleum deposits according to tested procedures; we conversely have a lower degree of faith in "historical" geology as spokesmen suppose fossils that are not found. We place faith in biology when a scientist tells us that our dog will have puppies, rather than kittens; we have a lower degree of faith in biology when someone tells us that human beings and monkeys had common ancestors.

In his foreboding scientific journal article,* physicist W. Jim Neidhart speaks eloquently to this very point. "Faith," he asserts is "a component of all human understanding." He continues:

> How can faith be a necessary component of scientific as well as religious experience? Let us first clearly understand that faith does not provide the data of empirical knowledge; faith rather plays its role in seeking to find a keystone idea, a pattern that will fit and explain the data. Science does not consist merely of the collecting of data; we must recognize what is truly coherent in what we observe, which observations are truly significant.

The writer gives a list of "faiths" that any scientist must hold to work in the sort of world we have:

> A scientist cannot begin his task of deciphering the puzzle of a very complex physical world without an unconditional and complete trust or conviction in certain basic premises that undergird all scientific effort. In essence he must possess a *firm faith* that nature is intelligible, that an underlying unique and neces-

*W. Jim Neidhardt, "Faith, The Unrecognized Partner of Science and Religion," *Journal of American Scientific Affiliation 26,* (September 1974), pp. 89-96. Quoted with permission.

sary order exists, that there is an ultimate simplicity and inter-
connectedness to the laws of nature, that underlying symmetries
exist in the physical world, that nature behaves in the same way
whether observed or not, that a direct, correct correspondence
exists between events of the universe and his sensory-brain re-
sponses, that his own sense and memory are trustworthy, and
finally that his fellow workers do and report their work honestly.

"To doubt or engage in endless questioning of such points,"
Neidhardt goes on, "is to abandon the whole purpose of scientific
pursuit." He concludes that:

Faith coupled with observation and deduction, not merely observation and deduction, is required for progress in science . . .
The condition of the scientist and the man of religion are in this
respect the same. Religious faith stems from its own evidences,
exactly as that of the scientist; it is not blind faith.

Dr. Neidhardt explained the animosity between the scientific
community and the "humanistic" community in general:

A deep cleavage exists today between the scientific and religious
communities, between scientists and humanists in general. The
goals, methods, and problems of one group are considered ir-
relevant, of no interest and significance by the other. Communication between the two groups is at times almost
completely lacking.

But the writer thinks the situation could be greatly helped by a
good look at the very foundations of both communities:

The history of science, past and present, shows that both the
sciences and the humanities have at their center some common
mental attitudes. One of them perhaps the most significant, is
man's dependence, as he creatively seeks to understand all of
reality, on his "firm and solid feelings," on his faith. Faith is a
valid component of all human knowledge, scientific as well as
religious.

The writer concludes the article with a call to everyone to stop regarding science as "a cold, analytical discipline devoid of faith," and to Christians to stop "completely compartmentalizing their perspectives of the spiritual and natural orders . . . Faith correctly viewed is that illumination by which true rationality begins . . ." That last statement brought me up short. I had been guilty of both bad habits the good scientist had cited in his conclusion; I had been thinking of science as cold and devoid of faith of any sort, and I had certainly compartmentalized my own perspectives of the spiritual and natural orders.

I had started out my questioning of Dr. John Moore by frankly confessing that I had been a weekday evolutionist and a Sunday creationist. Now, I was ending my study with a scientist's call to come out of my closet.

I did.

I now believe creation. And I have reasons.

I had been almost convinced of creation after John took me on his "evolution trip" and "creation trip," but I had still been troubled by the issue of faith. If both evolution and creation required faith, why should the faith in one be better than the faith in the other? Well, I had an answer to that one now. The faith connected with creation is better, to me, because it's based on a more reliable source. I personally trust the Scriptures more than I trust the scenario-making men, and now that I know that evolution is really only scenario-making, I reasonably opt for creation.

Perhaps I would have arrived at the same place even if I didn't "have religion." I understand that some people who don't call themselves "religious," believe the world was created; they just can't swallow evolution.

Besides a comparison of faiths between creation and evolution, I also had the comparison of observable data which Dr. Moore had supplied. And there I think creation wins hands down. Genetics, embryology, and other areas all seem consistent with creation and contradictory to evolution.

I now became very interested in the public debate over creation and evolution. Now I had a new cause, because John had explained the results of the teaching of evolution. I have a son in high school. I've never thought he descended from animals and I really don't want anyone to tell him that he has.

I didn't feel strongly about this when I was a closet evolutionist, of course. I asked Dr. Moore to send me "the works" about the public debate and he laid it on thick. He sent facts and history, and he included his own public debate with a qualified scientist as it appeared in a state teachers' journal.

The following chapter is a distillation of the material Dr. Moore sent me.

6
The Public Debate

In recent decades teachers in American public schools have taught only the evolution model of origins. In some schools, it was taught soon after Darwin, a century ago. Today it's a rare event to find a public school teacher, however morally or ethically oriented, or however scientifically exact, who mentions the alternative of the creation model of origins.

But a David-and-Goliath battle has been ensuing in various American states where concerned parents, scientists, and legislators have protested the exclusivity of the teaching of evolution. To date, the Texas, Michigan, Ohio, Georgia, Washington, Oregon, Colorado, Tennessee, and California state legislatures have been the scene of struggles between the creation and evolution sectors.

There's quite a bit of passion to the debate. Compare these two statements by spokesmen of the evolution and creation sectors respectively:

> Antiscientism (the spokesman's term for creation) can only succeed by means of the apathy or the ignorance of those most concerned. It is discouraging to note how many scientists and educators are uninformed about fundamentalist activities in their own regions . . . Many scientists are apathetic because they regard the situation as ridiculous or incredible. They cannot be-

lieve that a 100-year-old argument has again surfaced in a serious and meaningful fashion. (But) this is a well-financed, well-organized campaign that is quite capable of success unless the scientific and educational communities react vigorously.*

[Evolution] is not harmless. It has been shown repeatedly that evolution is a keystone in the philosophy of atheism. It carries a tremendous responsibility for the loss of faith, the breakdown of moral standards, and the lack of purpose so sadly evident during the past century . . . Why protest? Because the teaching of evolution as proven fact in our schools and universities is technically unsound and philosophically damaging. Because if you, as a parent, do not want materialistic philosophies pumped into your children—or you, as a student, do not want to be brainwashed with atheism—some protesting voice must be heard.†

The Legal Battle

The legal debate goes back to the famous Scopes trial. According to a 1925 Tennessee law, evolution could not be taught in the public schools. A few months after the law was passed, John Thomas Scopes, a young science teacher in Dayton, was indicted for teaching evolution, tried, and fined $100 in the Dayton court. The decision was appealed to the state supreme court, and in 1927 Scopes was cleared on a technicality but the constitutionality of the law was upheld.

The Scopes trial is over, but the dust it raised has not yet settled.

California is a case in point that demonstrates how heated the battle between creationists and evolutionists can become. Associate members of the Creation Research Society began their efforts there in 1963, and they "fought a good fight." For six years they petitioned the State Board of Education in California to allow the creation account also to be taught in the schools. Finally, in 1969, a document known as the "Science Framework for California Public Schools" was issued, which allowed for some discus-

---

* William Mayer, "Evolution and the Law" *The American Biology Teacher* (March 1973), pp. 144-145.
† A. G. Tilney, "Why Protest about Evolution?" Supplement to Evolution Protest Movement Gazette (Australia) August 1973.

sion. Two Board members sought to amend the document to include some allusion to creation; a *Los Angeles Times* editorial covered the proceedings and citizens began to show an interest.

A private citizen, Vernon L. Grose, an aerospace engineer, read the editorial and submitted an interesting middle-ground view to the Board. Grose was not necessarily partisan to either creation or evolution, but as a scientist he had something to say about what is accurate in teaching origins.

Two of Grose's paragraphs seemed so reasonable to the Board members that they excised the passages of the "Framework" that dealt with evolution and replaced them with Grose's version. Grose said this:

> All scientific evidence to date concerning the origin of life implies at least a dualism or the necessity to use several theories to fully explain the relationships between established data points. This dualism is not unique to this field of study, but is also appropriate in other scientific disciplines such as the physics of light.
>
> While the Bible and other philosophical treatises also mention creation, science has independently postulated the various theories of creation. Therefore, creation in scientific terms is not a religious or philosophic belief. Also note that creation and evolutionary theories are not necessarily mutual exclusives. Some of the scientific data (e.g. the regular absence of transitional forms) may be best explained by a creation theory, while other data (e.g. transmutation of species) substantiate a process of evolution.

"War" Was Declared

The committee of scientists who originally prepared the "Framework" document completely repudiated the revised version because of the substitution of the two paragraphs. Board members stuck to the new version, however, and the National Association of Biology Teachers joined the fray. They raised funds for the legal defense of any teacher who might have gone afoul of the "Framework" as he taught evolution, and they submitted any number of protests and resolutions from various scientific societies for the Board to reconsider the revised version. Members of The National Academy of Science submitted one such protest.

The creationist Board members appointed citizen Grose to their Curriculum Development and Supplemental Materials Commission, a body that selects materials for approval by the State Board of Education.

In 1972 a curious situation developed concerning a biology textbook produced by a national publisher. The book was issued with two different covers—a national edition and a California edition. The national edition pictures evolutionary paleoanthropologist L.S.B. Leakey on the cover to illustrate an account of man's origins; the California edition shows Michelangelo's "Creation of Adam." *Science* magazine dryly reported, "The switch of Adam for Leakey accurately symbolizes the two sides of a controversy that has engulfed the teaching of science in California's elementary schools." *

The same issue of *Science* also reported a rather remarkable hearing before the State Board in preparation for adoption of textbooks for the schools. "Witnesses from each side appeared in each other's clothing—the creationists claiming to speak in the name of science, and the evolutionists in the name of biology and religion. The evolutionist side fielded both a Mormon bishop and the dean of San Francisco's Grace Episcopal Cathedral, who argued the primacy of science over Genesis as strongly as any evolutionist could have wished."

Vernon Grose continued to argue his moderate but insistent position in favor of including creation, describing evolution and creation as, "the case for chance" and "the case for design," respectively. "His views," stated the same issue of *Science,* "seem to be shared in part by aerospace acquaintances of his such as Wernher von Braun and Apollo astronauts Jim Irwin and Edgar D. Mitchell." Grose said, in an interview with the magazine, that he was concerned that "school children, brought up to believe there is a God, are now told in the name of science that God has conclusively been shown to be out of the picture. I want that to be withdrawn and a neutral or pro-theistic account to be given."

"If a child raises questions about the creator posited in the creation theory," Grose told the interviewer, "the teacher should reply that science knows nothing for or against a creator. Science has overstepped its limits by treating of first causes, science

---

* Nicholas Wade, "Creationists and Evolutionists: Confrontation in California," *Science,* Vol. 178, No. 4062, November 17, 1972, pp. 724-728, 729.

has been oversold in Western culture as the sole repository of objective truth."

Grose believed, according to the *Science* article, that the change he sought to bring about "will be a change that ranks with when we ceased to believe the earth was flat."

There is not sufficient space to document all of the later developments in the California battle, but suffice it to say that, though creation is now an alternative in some schools there, the fight continues.

The Battles Out of Court

In 1970 Dr. Moore and Harold Schultz Slusher, with 18 associate writers under sponsorship of the Creation Research Society completed the textbook *Biology: A Search for Order in Complexity* (Zondervan Publishing House, Grand Rapids, Mich., Second Edition, 1974). The book, according to the publisher, is "factually accurate and comprehensive, yet noticeably nonconventional in its approach . . . renders a refreshing alternative to most high school biology textbooks currently in use. This highly readable, teachable text examines the evidences for evolution as a theory of origins. But at the same time it explicitly presents biblical creationism as the most reasonable and satisfying explanation for the facts of biology as we know them today. An excting breakthrough for biological study in the classroom of the '70s."

Textbooks alone won't win the battle, of course, nor will the adoption of state rulings like those in California. The approach to any given topic in a classroom is still in the hands of the individual teacher. John's final concern, after he has helped with the legal battle and edited the textbook, is simply, "Who's going to implement it?"

What Board of Education rulings and the textbooks *can* do, however, is give any biology teacher the legal right to offer the creation model of origins in his classroom. Things have nearly reversed since the classroom of John Thomas Scopes, and without the various state board rulings, a biology teacher today could conceivably have to stand trial for the teaching of creation! Such a situation would demonstrate the endless virility of this argument.

A relatively small minority of creationists continues to spread the word of creation through speaking engagements, new articles, and debates with evolutionists who are willing to take up the challenge. School teachers ask for copies of the book to become informed about the other side. Parents approach school officials about placing textbook and other creation materials in the school libraries.

The Institute for Creation Research (ICR), of which John is a member of the Technical Advisory Board, now sponsors Creation Seminars for teachers, parents, and pastors in order to promulgate the doctrine of creation in the schools. The establishment of Christian Heritage College and ICR, the research division of the college, in 1970 "marked for the first time in history, as far as is known, that an educational and research center was founded strictly on creationist principles and purposes."

A landmark was also reached July 10, 1975, the fiftieth anniversary of the Scopes trial, when the *New York Times* printed a story which mentioned the creationists. The article called them "objectors."

The "objectors" are steadily getting more attention as the public debate continues. In the professional journal *Perspectives in Biology and Medicine* (spring 1975) Dr. John A. Moore, an evolutionist, referred to the "influential creationists." Creationists used to be called "fanatical."

The Michigan Science Teachers Bulletin, published by the Michigan State Teachers Association, devoted part of the Winter 1974 issue to the creation-evolution debate which had begun in force in Michigan. Dr. Moore (John N.) argued for the inclusion of the creation model in the school curriculum; Dr. Jerome S. Miller, instructor in biology at Grand Rapids Junior College (Grand Rapids, Mich.), argued for the exclusion of creation.

These articles, in excerpted portions, and the introduction by W.C. Van Deventer, editor of the *Bulletin* are printed here by special permission. The entire articles are available from the Michigan State Teachers Association, Michigan State University, East Lansing, Mich. 48823.

EVOLUTION IN THE SCHOOLS
W. C. Van Deventer
Editor, *Michigan Science Teachers Bulletin*

The writer was in high school at the time of the Scopes evolution trial in 1925. This trial came about as a result of the passage of a law by the State of Tennessee making it illegal to teach evolution in the public schools. Scopes was a high school biology teacher who was willing to take part in a test case in the courts. The famous orator and fundamentalist churchman, William Jennings Bryan, assisted the prosecution. The equally famous attorney, Clarence Darrow, headed the case for the defense. Bryan died of a heart attack during the trial and the results were inconclusive. Later the law was repealed.

There was, of course, a much earlier controversy in the learned world following the publication of Charles Darwin's *The Origin of Species* in 1859. Thomas Henry Huxley, Bishop Wilberforce of the Anglican Church, and other famous 19th-century names were associated with it.

The work of the Biological Sciences Curriculum Study in the late 1950s and early 1960s, in producing modern texts for the teaching of high school biology, took the position that it is time high school teachers stopped spending their time and their students' time "proving" that evolution has taken place in the world of life, and instead studied how evolution has taken place. All three BSCS Color Versions are written from this viewpoint.

The writer has been teaching biology since the late 1920s. He has always approached the teaching of evolution from the standpoint of students learning *how* it has taken place, rather than simply proving *that* it has taken place. This point of view holds essentially that evolution is amply proved, that it is a going concern rather than just something which took place in the distant past, and that it is a phenomenon which is observable in the study of the things that man uses as well as in the world of life. In the writers's classes, therefore, we teach the evolution of language, clothing, the automobile, and other man-made things as well as the evolution of living organisms. This presents the idea of evolution in a broad and less controversial framework.

Recently, the teaching of evolution in the schools has again become a matter of controversy (if, indeed, it ever ceased to be so). The State of California has a law requiring the teaching of the "creation theory" along with the "evolution theory." The editor has been under considerable pressure to devote an issue of the *Bulletin* to this problem. Therefore, he has asked two good friends of his to contribute articles on the subject for publication. Dr. John N. Moore of Michigan State University is nationally known for his position as a proponent of creation as opposed to evolution. Dr. Jerome S. Miller of Grand Rapids Junior College is a teacher of long standing and is well-known for his scholarly presentation of biology. The editor wishes to express his appreciation to these two writers for the privilege of presenting the problem in their words at this high level.

SHOULD CREATION BE TAUGHT
IN PUBLIC SCHOOLS?
Jerome S. Miller, Ph.D.

Within the past few years, a controversy has arisen concerning the teaching of evolution, first in California, later in Colorado, Georgia, and Tennessee, and now in Michigan, with demands for equal time for presentation of "creation theory" in public secondary schools. That such an issue should arise in the space age as the 20th century draws to a close seems incredible to those of us professional teachers who thought that these matters had long ago been settled by the Scopes trial of the 1920s.

Fast-breaking discoveries in molecular biology, the revelation of the DNA code, intriguing research in support of the heterotroph hypothesis of the origin of life, more than idle speculation about life on other planets, and the exciting resurrection of the theory of continental drift—all these accumulations of data are well on their way to solidifying the theory of evolution as the only scientifically plausible explanation for the diversity of life on earth, both past and present.

One can only marvel at the motivation of those seeking equal time, by law or decree, for so-called "creation theory." It may be a manifestation of the anti-intellectual tenor of the times, a reflection of the back-to-nature movement in reaction to the social problem technology has brought about in human society, and a wistful longing to return to a simpler time and way of thinking. For years, passionate anti-evolutionists have blamed evolutionary teaching for all the moral ills that beset us, claiming erosion of religious faith. Perhaps these same forces are now at work in a more subtle form. It is very tempting to place one's trust in an all-seeing, knowing, caring, wise deity in search for immorality and inner peace. True scientists are none the less human for all their training, but do not let their emotions interfere with their thinking. Wishful thinking is not science.

For those who may not have kept track of the controversy, most of the facts and arguments have appeared in *The American Biology Teacher,* a publication familiar to and available to most teaching biologists. From November 1970 to May 1973, some 25 articles, editorials, and letters have been published. Similar articles and reports have also appeared in the *N.A.B.T. News and Views,* a publication of the National Association of Biology Teachers which became so alarmed at the threat to academic freedom that they established a fund for freedom in science teaching.

The issue began in California and has snowballed to other states. The California State Board of Education was the instigator, and the legislatures in other states have entertained either bills or constitutional amendment proposals. In Michigan an attempt was made during the waning months of 1972 but the bill died with adjournment. In early 1973, a newspaper dispatch dated January 31 states, "Bills requiring schools which teach the evolutionary theory of man's origins to also teach the Biblical Story were introduced in the Michigan Senate Tuesday. The new bills were sponsored by Sens. James Fleming of Jackson and Gary Byker of Hudsonville. The bills require teachers who teach evolution to devote a reasonable amount of time to teaching the Biblical version as a history version of the subject." As I write this in July, the legislature is tied up with budgetary matters and I have seen no word as to the fate of these bills.

Should Michigan teachers be concerned? Definitely yes, if you teach in a secondary school. Teaching in community colleges and the four-year colleges and universities would not be affected. Could this come about, if not this year then possibly the next? Listen to William Mayer writing in the March 1973 issue of *The American Biology Teacher.*

"The independent status of many governmental agencies allows them to promulgate rules or regulations that, in terms of their designated interest, have the force of law. The California State Board of Education, for example, is appointed by the governor and is virtually autonomous in dealing with public education (four-year colleges excepted) in that State,—such agencies have great power; and, because they are not directly responsible to either the public or the legislature, they create a situation wherein a few willful men can control the agency and direct it to do their bidding."

He continues, "A different involvement with the law is, of course, the creation of law itself, primarily through legislative action. A recent example of this—occurred in 1972 when religious fundamentalists in Colorado managed to get support of six state representatives and six senators to introduce House Concurrent Resolution 1011 as an amendment to the state constitution." He quotes the resolution and following that comments, "In effect, the bill was saying that any state-supported institution that in any way dealt with the purposes of life, man, and the universe—which includes pretty much everything—would be required to provide time, space, and tax money to support fundamentalist presentations. I am pleased to say that I was a leader in organizing opposition to this bill, which would have set up fundamentalistic religion as state teaching policy and infringed on the academic freedom of every teacher in the state."

How did he do this? Mr. Mayer explains, "In order to defeat such measures they must be given maximum publicity, and this I attempted to do by writing to every institution of higher education in Colorado and by persuading scientists and educators to tell the members of the state legislature how they felt about the matter. One characteristic of persons who advocate such efforts (teaching of creation) is their desire to maintain a low profile and to use such catchy phrases as 'academic freedom' to indicate that theirs is a harmless and reasonable request. . . ."

Those interested in details should read the article in its entirety, but these few excerpts should be sufficient to alert the Michigan teaching community that complacency leads to control. The saddest aspect of this trend is the apparent abandonment of the persuasion of evangelism for the compulsion of law. Having failed to convert others by argumentation, fundamentalists persist in forcing their views on others by legal means using the shady trick of claiming equal time—a current favorite political concept. Their proposal would violate the principle of separation of church and state and it is to their discredit that they feel that the end justifies the means. For centuries overemotional fervor has stained the good name of religion as a human institution. The trial of Galileo should remind us all of the dangers of excess.

What did the news media think? *The Grand Rapids Press* editorially condemned the 1972 bill, and on March 22, 1973, *The Ann Arbor News* had this to say, "In Michigan as in California, legislation is afoot to require equal time to the schools for the teaching of the biblical account of creation. Equal time in this case means balancing out the teaching of evolution with the story of Genesis. There really isn't any need to add to the clutter on the statute books, but it might also tangle the schools in the church-state thicket. Let's leave well enough alone. A reasonable compromise is for teachers in public schools to stress the theory of evolution, emphasis on the theory. A growing body of scientific opinion already is casting doubts on evolution, but let's not get into that. Suffice it to say that teachers may offer evolution, as one theory for man's origins and let it go at that,— as a theory."

Before we consider the "doubts" mentioned in the editorial, further comment on the legal and ethical problems is in order. While our pledge of allegiance states, "One nation, under God, . . ." it doesn't specify which God. Of course a Christian or Jewish God is assumed, and perhaps Allah would be acceptable, but what of all the other deities of the many and varied religions of the world? Are they to be denied equal time on the grounds that the Christian religion is the one true account? Truly, one religion's truths may be another religion's myths, and we quickly brand as superstitions all beliefs in conflict with our own. To teach the biblical account of creation would be to presume that this is the only valid account that is acceptable, and one can only hope that advocates of this view are prepared to offer proof that their version is supported by scientific evidence as inherent in their use of the term "theory" in the phrase "creation theory."

Proponents of the Judaeo-Christian concept of creation appear to advocate that simple reading of the Bible is sufficient. Certainly, the details of their presentation have not been forthcoming. If their contention is that it is truly "creation theory," a term that gives it the cloak of academic respectability, then they should be willing and able to provide hard evidence to substantiate their claim. Some of the best thinkers, both philosophers and theologians, have given this their attention throughout the ages and the matter is far from settled. . . .

I would like to close with one more quote from a concerned source. Jerry Lightener in an editorial in the *American Biology Teacher* for January 1973 states the problem clearly. Read, and ponder your own situation.

Mr. Lightener says in part, "I submit that scientists and science educators have had only mediocre success in communicating the dimensions, limitations, and requirements of science. The general population and possibly too many science teachers, do not understand the nature of scientific theory. I would also suggest that they do not understand the nature of philosophic thought and religious belief. Science and religion both have their place in a liberal education. But it is foolhardy to attempt to equate scientific theory with religious faith; they simply are not amenable to the same judgments and tests. Science textbooks are not science textbooks when creation-by-design is treated as a scientific theory. Until a creation *theory* is developed that tends to be confirmed by widespread, rigorous investigation, it has no place in a science textbook."

This article has been written from one teacher to another. Granted that I as a community college instructor would likely be unaffected by legislation, I am still concerned in that my colleagues would be responsible for the instruction of pupils who may enter my classes, and might be forced to exceed their special expertise and enter a twilight zone for which they may be unprepared. Should creation be taught in public schools? Considering the aforegoing metaphysical argument would you be qualified to teach it? Would tenth grade pupils understand it at that level? You be the judge. Mr. Mayer has told you what action blocks legislative compulsion. Now it's up to you.

EVOLUTION, CREATION, SCIENTIFIC METHOD, AND LEGISLATION
by John N. Moore, M.S., Ed. D.

This Twentieth Annual Convention of the Michigan Science Teachers Association is dedicated to the motto: "Quest for Quality." I agree. Let there be a quest for quality in science teaching. Just as there has been a "call" for truth in advertising, and a "call" for truth in lending, so let there be a "call," here and now, for truth in science teaching. . . .

I have shown, in careful itemized fashion, that evolution, a "Molecules to Man," is without any empirical basis. Let it be taught thus to young and old at all levels of the educative enterprise. It is highly incredible that a speculative, imaginative narrative regarding supposed evolutionary origins of animals, plants, and human beings could have been universally adopted and taught as scientific fact in all public schools. Rather evolution is essentially a philosophy, a world view, or a frame of reference by which all living things, especially man, are seen in perspective to the whole of the universe.

As a summary to what I have said so far, it must be clear that evolution has never been proved as a scientific fact; has never been substantiated by any laboratory experiments. Evolution, therefore, is neither fact nor hypothesis nor theory. It is a belief, a faith, and nothing more. Of course, like evolution, creation is not accessible to the scientific method. Concepts about origins and events that are not presently observable, because they are not repeatable, are involved in both evolution and creation.

However, evolution *and* creation can be formulated as conceptual *models,* or frameworks, with which men can correlate facts and even make predictions. Yet, neither model can be proved; neither model can be tested directly. The evolution model and the creation model can only be compared in terms of the relative ease with which they can be used to explain data which exist in the real world.

Yet, creation is actually a far more effective model for correlating scientific data than evolution; and, evolution requires a far more credulous religious faith in the illogical and unprovable than does creation. An abundance of sound scientific literature is now available to document this statement, but few evolutionists have bothered apparently to read much of it.

What can science teachers do? I suggest they admit that there are sound scientific and pedagogical reasons why *both* models should be taught, as objectively as possible, in public classrooms whenever teachers and students are discussing origins. They can teach with care so that arguments pro and con for each model are clearly expressed. Such treatment is necessary for minimum, basic compliance with academic freedom. But, also, this pro and con approach is required since some students and their parents believe in creation, some believe in evolution, and some are undecided in their beliefs.

If creationists desire only the creation model be taught, then they should send their children to private schools which do this; if evolutionists want only evolution to be taught, then they should provide private schools for that purpose. However, the public schools should be neutral and science teachers should either teach both models or teach neither model of origins. Such is the clearly equitable and constitutional approach.

Further, I suggest that no one need "fear" about violation of "separation of church and state", *if such equitable treatment abounds.* Court decisions restricting "religious" teaching in the public schools do not apply to "creation" teaching about origins.

On the contrary, a case could be presented very well that violation of revered separation of church and state has occurred already by means of the now established, exclusive manner in which science teachers in the state of Michigan, and across the land, have selectively indoctrinated students at various educative levels into *only one model,* that is, the evolution model. The predominant "religion" of naturalism and humanism so commonly applied by science teachers during discussions of origins has been, in effect, the established religion of the State for a hundred years. Indication of this exclusive position is evidenced when creationists propose that the creation model be taught in the public schools along with the evolution model. Evolutionists commonly react emotionally, rather than scientifically.

How, then, can student rights be protected? Does the School Code of Michigan protect the academic freedom of science teachers who want to prevent selective indoctrination of their students by presenting both the evolution model and the creation model of origins? Are principals and superintendents of public schools appropriately aware that science teachers who present both models are giving their students the better educative experience? Are principals and superintendents themselves mindful whether the School Code of Michigan protects the academic freedom of science teachers and in turn the civil rights of students?

I believe that many teachers and administrators are quite willing to present both viewpoints, but have been unaware that a solid scientific case for creation exists, and, therefore, they do not know how to present both viewpoints. There is thus a great need for teachers, room libraries, and school libraries to be supplied with sound creationist literature. Perhaps some schools, or even districts, will be willing to provide such literature. I suggest that, if sound creationist books are conveniently available, many teachers (not all, unfortunately, but far more than at present) would be willing to use such resource materials and to encourage their students to use them.

Or, is there need for legislative intervention in strengthening the School Code of Michigan? Are legislators doing their duty as elected officials of the taxpayers, that is parents, when they consider bills whereby the School Code of Michigan may be explicated as affording just the necessary protection for science teachers and students, such that selected indoctrination not occur and true academic freedom is obtained?

Is there a logical role for parents? In this State parents are still fully responsible for the education of their children under the School Code. They are required to send their children to school, public or private. Is their responsibility properly exercised through attention to how the subject of origins is treated by science teachers? It would seem totally in keeping with parental responsibilities that contact with their legislators for assistance in *clarifying* the School Code of Michigan is orderly and proper.

Today parents are becoming more and more aware through mass communication media of the scientific literature that is available to document the position that the creation model is scientifically effective as a tool to explain origins. Also, many parents are fully aware of the fallacious nature of the evolution model, and of the various compromising positions, such as theistic evolution, day-age concepts, gap concepts, local flood plans, etc.

Therefore, parents can hold informative discussions with officials at high levels (State education boards, district boards, superintendents, etc.) to acquaint them with the evidences that can be used to support the creation model and the importance of the issue. School officials can be requested to inform the science teachers of the State or district that the equal teaching of the evolution model and the creation model, not on a religious basis, but as models which can be used to correlate scientific data, is both permitted and encouraged.

Cases of unfair discrimination against creationist minorities in classrooms can be reported, and most school officials at such levels are sufficiently concerned and sensitive to the needs of all their constitutents that, if they can first be shown there is a valid scientific case for the creation model and that evolution has at least as much religious character as does creation, they will quite probably favor such a request, that is, a request for equitable treatment of both models regarding origins.

Again, what can science teachers do? I recommend that science teachers can serve their own responsibility as public servants, as teachers of young formative minds, by putting their own "house in order", *before* parents and legislators seize the initiative to protect the civil rights and academic freedom of students and science teachers alike. Science teachers can take advantage of already available reference books, textbooks, laboratory materials, supplementary textbooks, films, and film strips which have been prepared by other scientists. Science teachers can take advantage of a type of in-service training through seminars and summer institutes that have been inaugurated in many states in recent years.

I suggest and recommend that now is the time for all good science teachers to come to the aid of the "Quest for Quality" in science teaching regarding origins. The responsibility and initiative should rest most properly with science teachers. Any study of origins is a vital part of the field of speciality of the science teacher.

Science teachers arise, put your "house in order" by teaching

BOTH the evolution model *and* the creation model of origins, so that you protect the civil rights and also the academic freedom of your students *and* your own rights and academic freedom, as well.

When most furious, the creation-evolution debate leads to accusations from both sides, with some pretty serious charges. Evolutionists tend to characterize the opposition as intolerant, backward, and sneaky. They seem to think of creationists as sacrificing true science on the altar of their particular religious convictions. Creationists, for their part, characterize the evolutionists as unscientific—promoting a purely imagined belief system—and overly insistent on a hopeless humanism which has led to a decline of moral values.

On the issue of the venerated American principle of the separation of church and state, both sides accuse the other of violating this principle. Evolutionists violate it by insisting on teaching the basis of atheism—a faith system—say the creationists; creationists violate separation by insisting on teaching the existence of God—another system of belief—say the evolutionists.

A Summary

Dr. Moore gave me the following wrap-up of the public debate as he saw it.

Dr. Moore:

Today a majority of leading scientists, particularly biologists, do not want parents to pay any attention to how their children (whether at elementary, high school, or even college and university levels) are instructed about the origins of things.

Leading biologists are actually reluctant to "practice what they preach" in their discipline, which involves a real commitment to the concept that all ideas are open to reexamination and retesting.

For at least the last century, most school curriculums have included presentation of the so-called "evolutionary" view of the first origin of the universe, of life, of humankind. During that time no careful discussion of the biblical position of first origins has been presented in textbooks.

Such "evolutionary" ideas have been taught exclusively—essentially without challenge. Even the Scopes trial just 50 years ago was not a real challenge, since participants did not engage in any specific examination of pros and cons regarding data in biology, geology, and embryology.

Nevertheless, since 1964, parents in California, Texas, Tennessee, Ohio, Indiana, Michigan, and state after state have expressed criticisms about educational experiences in public schools, especially when they felt that their children's values and beliefs were being altered undesirably.

And since 1972 editors of some scientific journals have recognized that a minority of scientists have supplied parents with concrete information to challenge the dominant, even dogmatic, "evolutionary" teachings about first origins to their children.

Particular attention is increasing with regard to the help parents receive from articles published in the *Creation Research Society Quarterly* (available from 2717 Cranbrook Road, Ann Arbor, MI 48104 at $8 a year). Authors in the *Quarterly* are pointing out the "bankruptcy" of terminology used by "evolutionary" writers in such important publications as *The American Biology Teacher, Science,* and *Scientific American.*

In these scientific journals, authors utilize such terms as "could," "might," "suppose," "suggest," and "expected" with regard to ideas of first origins, which are absolutely untestable, and hence are outside of solid scientific investigation.

Even the word *scenario* is used as authors in *Science* have *imagined* aspects of the origin of the moon. Since when has scenario writing, i.e., playwriting, become a part of *scientific* endeavor?

To cut through the "bankruptcy" of terms used by evolutionists, this writer maintains regularly in public addresses that evolutionists include supernatural—supra-natural or beyond the natural—in their thinking.

Evolutionists use the supernatural in their thinking about some "big bang" that started the universe.

Evolutionists use the supernatural in their thinking about spontaneous generation of first life at the sub-microscopic level of organization.

Evolutionists use the supernatural in their thinking about movement of dry rock masses in supposed mountain building.

Evolutionists use the supernatural in their thinking about some initial continental drift whereby present land masses supposedly came into existence.

Evolutionists use the supernatural in their thinking about accidental mutational changes (errors) in other kinds of organisms as a source presumably of humankind.

To sum it all up, I want to emphasize that evolutionists have been teaching a purely *imagined* belief system about first origins in the public schools at most levels for the last three decades, if not for the last 100 years. I hold that the late Julian Huxley and his sycophantish followers in the public schools, with their "evolutionary" humanistic faith, are the ones who have been violating the so-called separation of church and state.

Parents rightfully criticize school systems wherein teachers of their children are guilty of selective indoctrination of the young into one belief system about origins, *at taxpayers' expense*—especially so, if that belief system is diametrically opposite to beliefs about first origins taught in the home.

7

Option for a Scientist

Now there were just two more questions I wanted to ask Dr. Moore. First, I wanted him to explain why he believed in creation. Second, I wanted to know if other people could believe in creation for the same reasons.

I knew the answers by this time, of course, but still I wanted to hear him say, "This is why . . ." and "Here's how you can, too." He obliged me with enough material for two chapters.

Dr. Moore Begins with Origins

I am a scientist.

I am well aware of what scientists have discovered about the possible first origins of the universe, the solar system, the earth, and the life thereon. I am also aware of what scientists have *not* found. I am aware of which questions remain unanswered by scientific investigation. These matters are my daily work.

Considering my position, the knowledge I have gathered and the limited state of inquiry into origins—I believe in creation.

It should be made clear that I choose the creation model of origins as a scientist, not as a religious zealot of any sort. I choose my position based on what is justified by known fact, not merely by what is taught in any church or school of theological thought. I highly respect different religious treatments of origins, but I take my own position with regard to origins based on the available facts.

I believe that the biblical account of origins, as given in the Book of Genesis (and enhanced throughout the Scriptures), is the only view that can be associated with any credible and reasonably acceptable pattern of thought when *all* known data are considered. The changing "theories" of men—plausible, interesting, and often in agreement with *certain* known data—have clearly been developed as conscious or unconscious substitutes for the Genesis account, and become highly questionable in the light of known scientific fact.

Considering for a moment the present ideas about the origin of the universe, and the solar system within it, there are three notions which are all very intriguing but are basically imaginative and without any indisputable evidence. The "steady-state theory," in which the universe has simply always "been here," rather disappoints the human mind. We are simply unfamiliar, to say the least, with ongoing processes that had no beginning. The "continuous creation" idea violates the principle of the second law of thermodynamics, according to which things are actually winding down. Nothing at all is being added to the closed system of the universe. We are a bit foolish to posit ideas that are counter to established scientific law. Only one of the two can be accurate, and the thermodynamics principles have been tested and verified.

Finally we have the "big-bang theory" of origins, in which we supposedly are part of an ongoing explosion of one former, very dense particle. This is a most imaginative exercise, entertaining us with a mental picture of a really *big* explosion. We are asked to believe that all detectable orderliness, both terrestial and celestial, has resulted from an "explosion." Incredible!

The three "theories," and others before those which have come and gone, simply are not supported by real observable replicable evidence; they are designed by men to roughly fit the few facts we have established about possible origins. That the three are mutually exclusive is manifested by the very nature of such "theories"; scientists will stand on one or the other of these ideas very firmly, but with the sure knowledge that an equally learned scientist from the next village holds a different view.

No "theory" of the origin of the universe better fits all data now known than does creation—the concise idea that the universe was purposely constructed by a divine Creator. The statement "In the beginning God . . ." has never been scientifically refuted.

The origin and continuity of life is another area of origins for which a Creator is required, in my view. Life is more than a mechanical system, and humankind—life that is aware of itself—very aptly agrees with a purposeful creation. But here too, men have posited extraordinarily imaginative but scientifically unsupported "theories" of origins.

Spontaneous generation has long been the general theme in men's ideas of the origin of life. Life is suposed to have begun, on some level, without any external intervention. There were, historically, the "theories" of macrozoic spontaneous generation (where whole organisms came into existence suddenly), then microzoic spontaneous generation (where the very small living things were generated in unaided fashion), and now, finally, in the present day, sub-microscropic spontaneous generation (where parts of molecules supposedly have been self-generated).

If spontaneous generation is granted, then presumably progress by evolution and steady improvement of life occurred. Somehow bigger and better forms of life emerged unaided from previous life. And the best result, so far, is man.

This involves in turn an imagined, complex interrelationship of living creatures, the principle of common ancestry. All animals, and man, finally, would be the latest production of some "family" of creatures which have previously "evolved." Man, therefore, would share common ancestry with animals.

The problem with this thinking is, again, evidence. In this case we do have some observable interrelationship of certain creatures; we know, for example, that a true mule has common ancestry with a horse and a donkey. But offspring of the horse and the donkey are mostly sterile and no herd of mules for breeding has been produced. And this simple case of strictly limited inter-breeding of living animals can hardly be evidence of the extraordinarily lengthy and erratic system of evolution from "simple" to complex forms of life.

Nor is any real evidence of common ancestry gained from ligers, or tiglons, that result from the inter-breeding of tigers and lions. No fertile offspring are known to have come from this cross; nor from the cross of the donkey and the zebra which yields offspring variously called zeedunks, zonkeys, and zebronkeys.

Furthermore, human beings have no common ancestry with any

other known organism. As human beings are known, they are known to have ancestry only with other human beings.

Evolutionists have tried to connect the human beings with various animal ancestries through tenuous similarities and vaguely corresponding characteristics. Vertebrates are said to be ancestors of men because of bone structures, for example, but then the analysts disagree as to where the vertebrates came from. Some have tried to trace vertebrates to insects; others to the earthworm or the jellyfish. Still others posit that vertebrates came from starfishlike organisms. In any case, no orderly progression whatever can be seen.

Fish and amphibians are widely supposed to have common ancestors; amphibians and reptiles presumably came next. Then we have reptiles and mammals with common ancestors, and finally mammals of some anthropoid nature (common with the ape or monkey?) are assumed to be ancestors of human beings.

It should be clearly understood that each of these steps represents pure imagination (and they are big steps, requiring big imaginations!) and that no such relationships are known. None have been observed and none are shown by experimentation. As I depend on observation and experimentation, especially in cases where experienced scientists disagree, I do not choose to believe the common ancestry thesis of the origin of life.

Objections to Scenarios

Much has been written and taught about the evolution model, as though repetition might make it true, but there is an acceptable way of scientific writing that is invariably violated by these reports. There is, after all, a difference betwen accurate reporting of sound scientific findings and stories about speculations. Good scientific reportage is characterized by specific attributes, such as cause-and-effect relationships and detection of uniformity of natural events in the environment. When assumptions are included they are identified as such. Testability of ideas given and of the existence of objects independent of the observer are important features.

This is a world apart from heaping suppositions upon suppositions. This latter characteristic, typical of writing according to the evolution model, is merely an exercise in speculative or creative writing, not scientific reportage. I am more used to basing my knowledge upon scientific reportage.

Scientific writing absolutely requires the reporting of materials and methods used in research; the procedures, techniques, and experiments utilized in arriving at the findings being presented; and the results, with tabulation of data and graphic presentation to aid the reader. Obviously all these criteria are missing in evolutionary writing.

Clearly, if an individual wishes to write about the origin of the moon, he will not be able to follow the above criteria of scientific writing; there are no experimental procedures for determining the origin of the moon. So, that article would not be scientific.

This does not necessarily mean that the article is invalid, uninteresting, or pointless. But it does mean that the ideas of the writer are merely ideas, not scientific fact. Origin-of-the-moon articles, in view of our present knowledge, are always "scenarios."

It has lately been fashionable, unfortunately, for "historical" geologists, evolutionary astronomers, biochemists, biologists, sociologists, and anthropologists, to do a great deal of scenario writing. This has become most popular as a field of creative writing, and the "findings" of the writers are packaged as home study courses and even as television "science" shows. These scenarios qualify well as entertainment but truth is perverted if they are taken as science. Thinking people must always draw the line between what has been established as scientific fact and what is posited by imaginative scenario fabricators.

Now you may ask if the creation story is not a scenario also. What are the procedures and experiments required to prove creation?

It's a fair objection, and we have already said in this book that no model of origins can be studied scientifically. Creation is not open to scientific investigation.

But my personal choice of creation is still based on the best of the proven scientific data that we *do* have. And it is fairly based also on the utter lack of probability of the other explanation of origins, the evolution model.

As a scientist I must fairly consider evolution as an option, and I have found in my considerations that it is unreasonable. Nothing regarding a "big bang" of some dense particle to start the universe is scientific or at all probable. Nothing regarding spontaneous generation of life on earth is scientific or at all probable. Nothing regarding chance, accidental changes of genes (that is, gene mutations occurring in some anthropoid forms) to suggest that mankind came from some animal origin is scientific or at all probable.

What I *do* understand scientifically are the laws of thermodynamics and the observable fixity of kinds among earthly life. The first law of thermodynamics (the conservation of matter and energy) and the second law (the continual running down of organized patterns) are most consistent with actions of a Creator. This, to me, is rational. And what I understand scientifically conflicts with the evolutionary model.

And I understand genetics and fossils and their consistency with the principle of fixity of kinds. Clearly, life does reproduce kind after kind; never does one species give rise to another species. To me, this fixity of kinds principle, in view of the striking similarities of skeletons, embryos, gross anatomy, and proteins, is all good evidence of a common plan that was utilized by an efficient Creator. Verily, the evidence is all around us and we are without excuse to believe in God, the Creator.

As a scientist, then, I can look on the one side of the question and find no experiments, no procedures for inquiry, no reportage beyond "scenarios"; on the other side I can apply proven scientific data to observable events. I have a clear choice, and I choose to make it.

The History of Scientific Work
Another way to approach the whole area of scientific investigation is to look at the history of scientific work. Obviously, scientists have come up with much useful, supported theory utilizing truly scientific methods. I have been interested in which sort of science produces which sort of results, based on my study of the procedures of successful scientists.

Bacon, Galileo, Kepler, and Newton carefully studied cause and effect and uniformity of events, and their basic work stands unchallenged by members of the scientific community and the rest of the world. We are deeply indebted to them. Their findings, the bases of much modern science, are among the most invaluable parts of the human heritage.

I find it interesting that they all believed in a Creator.

Linneaus, Mendel, Pasteur, Kelvin, and many others can be included in the large group of those whose work stands with the best scientific inquiry and who favored the biblical version of origins, complete with the Father and the Saviour. In some circles today these eminent scientists would be scoffed at, or their faith regarded as a human weakness. But their work in science attests to minds that would not be swayed by suppositions and scenarios; they still opted for the presently detested version of origins.

Kepler, whose studies helped lay the foundations of modern astronomy, would get laughs today for his singularly creationist view of his discoveries. But, without his work, many of those laughing would be helpless in their laboratories.

The tradition of believing scientists, then, is rather a proud one. Believing in God apparently does not harm one's ability.

Unbelieving scientists go back to a tradition of pagan thought which has changed little. We have referred to the ancient Greek tradition of debate for the sake of debate. The Greeks were clever scenario makers and we highly value their dramas; the stage is certainly the proper place for scenarios. But they struck upon evolution, too. (Never let it be thought that evolution is a modern concept; the thinkers of ancient times passed many amusing centuries contemplating it.)

The Greeks had various ideas about the atomistic nature of matter, about organization of the solar system (as per Eudoxus, Aristarchus, and Ptolemy), and about possible origins of life on earth. The Greeks and other early thinkers imagined that snakes came from horse hair, mice from mud, and flies from putrefying meat. They considered all the diverse life around them and they thought that diversity came from previous diverse life along some "chain of being" or some ladder of life. This was fairly good science for the times; some of the world, after all, had not yet come to a written language. But it is overwhelmingly discouraging to think that scenario making and the assigning of assumptions to unobservable events is *still* considered good science!

The history of science is indeed diverse on the question of origins. Believers can point back to believers, and pagans to pagans, even in the field of science. And we might say that each still reproduces after his own kind.

I don't mean to say, of course, that all the good scientists think one way and all the bad scientists another way. Actually, science is a mixed bag of philosophies where the Creator is concerned. Albert Einstein did not study the Bible and apparently knew no Saviour, but his special, intimate knowledge of the mechanics of the universe caused him to defend on many occasions the existence of the Creator. Observing what he did, Einstein believed in God.

That's my position too.

In the past, good scientists have never been willing to settle for "probabilities," and they have certainly never been willing to build secondary and tertiary probabilities upon original probabilities. This has never been science as we have known it. Like the believing scientists of the past, I have seen a glimpse of the universe and I believe in God, the Creator.

And that is, in a word, my final reason for believing the creation model. I understand some science and I find no accidental and highly improbable evolutionary system, but rather an organized, infinitely wonderful system of purposeful creation. I have met God in His creation.

Subjective Matters

I'll confess that revelation of God in His created universe is totally subjective. God *is* found in the laboratory, but only by the most serious of scientists. Creation is discovered by those unwilling to limit themselves to the suppositions of men and willing to inquire into what we see and what we experience. The history of science involved different kinds of scientists, as we have seen, and I opt for those whose work was unprejudiced by the imaginations of men.

There is a kind of repeatable "experiment" for discovering the Creator, and we will describe it in the following chapter. The Creator Himself has posed it, and it is available to all experimenters, assuming open minds.

In the meanwhile, suffice it to say that I still wear a white smock and bend over test tubes. I still study all sorts of science, and I still teach science in a major university. I have not grown wings and no one has observed a halo over my head. While it has been said of me that I am a fool to believe in God, this has not been verified scientifically.

I value the Bible as a scientifically accurate book, obviously, and I believe it implicitly. I anticipate no problems with biblical reportage on origins as scientific information is accumulated; it has survived thousands of years of new information and the biblical message remains intact and accurate.

I believe the *entire* message of the Bible, it should be said. I have not stopped my personal study of it with Genesis, though that book is most intriguing to me as a scientist. I am more than a mechanical creation—I have feelings. Thus I have read the rest of the Bible. I discovered my sinful nature and my need for salvation and discovered that provision has been made for this by the wise Creator who constructed the universe I live in. I have, of course, taken that provision to heart. I believe in Jesus Christ, who was a different kind of being than I am and is able to account for my behaving as I do when my behavior comes into question. My Creator has indicated that He will accept the work I have done for Him and the kind of creature I have been when I am ultimately represented by Jesus.

That is theology, some will say, not science. But remember, theology was once the "queen" of the sciences.

8

Conduct Your Own "Experiment"

In his doctoral studies, post-doctoral work, and 20 years of research, Dr. Moore has conducted two major "experiments."

First, he has tested both the evolution model and the creation model.

Dr. Moore began his scientific inquiries as an evolutionist, but he has become a creationist. He has looked deeply into both models of origins.

Initially, being the student of established scientists who believed in evolution, Dr. Moore took by faith their renditions of origins, and particularly the idea that Charles Darwin's *The Origin of Species* was really about the origin of the species. As a teacher in the natural sciences, he taught evolution. After a colleague confronted him with his teaching and the impact of it on his students, he began to read critically Darwin and other evolutionists. He was surprised and a bit disappointed to find that Darwin had studied the *variability* of the species but said nothing factual about their origin. In his book, Darwin indeed described many species, and numerous variations within those species, but the "proof" of evolutionary changes of living things was utterly lacking.

Moore began to notice, as he pursued his scientific research, that no real evidence for evolution existed. Despite a lack of evidence, it was taken for granted that the evolution model of origins was the true one, and most scientists simply worked within that "knowledge." Things lacking in evolution were characterized as "missing," "questions to be taken up later on," or "areas needing more research." Few scientists arrived at the idea that the evolution model was simply not true.

In his inquiries, Dr. Moore studied the results of experiments in genetic variation of life, fossils, and other standard "proofs" of evolution, and found no proof of evolution. What seemed to emerge was a pattern of purposeful creation, rather than a helter-skelter evolution based on mutations and changes across species.

Eventually Dr. Moore was exposed through serious study to the other version of origins—the Bible. He was not as likely as some scientists to throw the Bible away without reading it. He had heard that it contained myths and was merely the philosophical writings of men. But he applied to his reading of the Scriptures the same rigorous, objective testing that he applied to all inquiries.

Dr. Moore found the Bible reliable and accurate, in view of the data available about origins, and far superior to Darwin's work and all that followed along the lines of evolutionary thinking. He remains a Bible-believer with the question of origins completely settled in his mind.

Our purpose here is not to present the full testimony of Dr. Moore, but to point out that he has conducted the only available "experiment" about origins. Millions of others have conducted this "experiment" with reliable, predictable results. It is difficult to find cases of individuals who have conducted the "experiment" we are going to propose without getting the satisfactory answer experienced by Dr. Moore. Or, in other words, it is difficult to find a serious Bible-believer who questions that God is the origin of life, not to mention the destiny of life, including humankind.

The "experiment," Dr. Moore's second major "experiment," is a simple one, to be done in the following three steps.

1. Read the Bible and understand the basic message.
2. Act on that message.
3. Check the results.

As Bible-believers, we can give some guidance on these steps, but each man's commitment must be his personal decision. Dr. Moore has made this commitment.

Few people have read the entire Bible. The newer modern translations simplify the message, which is that God, the Creator, wishes to redeem men and women, His creatures.

Creation and the events between God and man present quite a different picture of life than evolutionists and many other kinds of learned men suppose, and it is important that we understand the highlights of that picture.

God created man perfectly, to begin with. The first man and woman were at first sinless, perfect creatures, and suitable company for a sinless, perfect God. But those human beings were created with free will, and they chose to exercise this free will in a negative way. Few people on earth are unaware of the story of the Garden of Eden and the Fall (Gen. 3), but even fewer appreciate the full impact of the story.

When men sinned, God, in effect, inaugurated a new plan. All of His subsequent plans were arranged to redeem man from that original fall and perfect him again for fellowship with his Creator. The plans involve a fascinating story of the choosing of a certain people—the Jews—through whom God reached the world in a special way: the life, death, and resurrection of His Son, Jesus Christ.

We have greatly simplified an enormous amount of biblical history, but through this we can see the basic message of the Scriptures which is useful to consider:

1. God made each man, purposefully.
2. Man is separated from God.
3. Jesus' sacrifice has reconciled this separation.
4. Each man must accept Jesus to be reconciled to God.

Those four principles (or "laws") have been put in many forms but the point is the same: there is a Creator and He loves the people He has made. Jesus Christ, God "in the flesh" ("Anyone who has seen Me has seen the Father" [John 14:9, LB]), came to be the sacrifice who would redeem humankind and make fellowship with the Creator possible again. Now this appears to be purely theological, but if there is a Creator at all, He is deeply interested in what He has made. We balk at the idea that the Creator who made the seas and the mountains, painted the wild flowers and designed the butterflies, simply wound the whole system up and left it running.

According to the first "law," God made everything with a purpose, and we discern that each man—God's ultimate creation—shares that purpose. We have a role in nature; each of us is important.

The evolutionary position on this contrasts discouragingly, each man being made accidentally, to no purpose. This appeals to some minds, to the basic nature of man. The constant, doctrinaire exposure to evolutionary ideas is a significant factor in affording human beings with excuses for their behavior patterns. They have been taught that human beings are just animals and thus many think in terms of using their fellows as means to their ends. Human beings are "experimented" with as in the artificial selection processes of some dictatorships. And further the survival and competitive concepts of evolutionists are used as an *excuse* to seize and possess the earth and natural resources and use them for the benefit of some and at the expense of others.

The second "law"—man is separated from God—entails the simple but profound truth behind all our struggles and troubles. Man was created with a will, the ability to make choices, and the majority of people have always chosen to oppose God. This independence from the Creator was illustrated early in man's history by Adam and Eve when they deliberately chose to oppose God.

In the creation model we see that the Creator had made perfection in the beginning. The animals and plants of the earth, with interdependent interlocking systems, were made with a symmetry and orderliness which even modern scientists depend on to function. We saw that the scientist, however he progresses and whatever his view of first origins, must have faith in this underlying orderliness of nature. But man has chosen to try to live outside of his originally created nature and act as if he were not dependent on his Creator.

According to the evolution model, man is not a dependent creature made by an intelligent Creator, of course, and thus men think they are free to wield nature for their own imagined betterment. The results of this thinking have been that man, initially given dominion over the earth and life on the earth, has dangerously polluted his environment, killed out abnormal numbers of other kinds, and found ways to utterly destroy his own kind. This modern age is a good time to think about that because we now stand seriously on the brink of simply wiping out everything.

The third "law"—that Jesus' sacrifice reconciles God and man

—is more than just a theological matter. Contemplation of the life of Jesus—even the spoken message of Jesus—reveals that He was no ordinary man. And repeatedly, in the midst of His profoundly knowledgeable assessment of the human condition, He asserted that He had been sent by the Creator. Redeeming men from their position of separateness from God—sin, in a word—was absolutely necessary, He said. He Himself proposed our "experiment" here when He advised simply, "Follow Me" (Luke 9:59).

His sacrifice, which He said would account for our sins and reestablish communion with the Creator, followed a principle of reconciliation to God apparent from the story of Cain and Abel. These sons of Adam and Eve offered sacrifices to God, by which they demonstrated their reverence toward Him and their dependence on Him. Specifically, Jesus became the ultimate sacrifice capable of redeeming all men.

In the evolution model, man is without a Creator or a purpose and thus cannot fall short of any standard. No Saviour of men is needed, and though the course of the entire human race seems destructive today, the evolutionist assumes constant improvement of life and a presumably better future.

The fourth "law"—each man must accept Jesus to be reconciled to God—stands to reason from the other three. If all of our troubles have been caused by our estrangement from our Creator, and if a method of reconciliation has been provided, we must certainly participate in that method. It is not enough for men to consider the reconciliation effective without personal participation any more than it fills our stomachs to know our fields are planted. Each man must personally eat to survive, and Jesus used this figure when He referred to Himself as "the bread of life" (John 6:35).

Each person is individually responsible to seek reconciliation with the Creator through Jesus Christ, according to the Scriptures. And we are assured, "Seek and ye shall find" (Matt. 7:7).

Finding Jesus is not difficult—He is available. Making a creature with a need and then not supplying that need is uncharacteristic of our Creator. The plant and animal worlds attest to that. Believers in Jesus Christ attest to that. Dr. Moore can attest to that. In 1962 (he remembers the exact date), he invited Him into his life.

Jesus is available "for the asking." Prayer is not often spoken of in the scientific community, but if our reckoning of the essence of the Scriptures is true, people need to speak to God.

It is not necessary to beseech God about reconciliation; He does not need to be begged for what He has already provided. When a man is convinced of the existence of God and of the need to be reconciled with Him, he simply asks for that reconciliation. "Ask, and it shall be given you . . . Knock and it shall be opened unto you" (Matt. 7:7).

In the evolution model this kind of activity is foreign indeed, and unnecessary. But now is the time to say that we have seen little moral satisfaction or human improvement from this debilitating view of life. Salvation by evolution, presumably depending on man's technological knowledge to solve our drastic problems, is by all evidences utterly hopeless.

But, millions of people have experienced the salvation of God through Jesus Christ that leads to the abundant life He promised (John 10:10).

Conduct your own "experiment." You'll be amazed at the results!

For Further Reading

Barnes, Thomas G. *Origin and Destiny of the Earth's Magnetic Field.* San Diego: Institute for Creation Research, 1973.

Clark, R.T. and Bales, James D. *Why Scientists Accept Evolution.* Nutley, N.J.: Presbyterian and Reformed Publishing Company, 1966.

Coppedge, James. *Evolution: Possible or Impossible?* Grand Rapids, Mich.: Zondervan Publishing House, 1973.

Custance, Arthur C. *Genesis and Early Man.* Grand Rapids, Mich.: Zondervan Publishing House, 1975.

Custance, Arthur C. *Noah's Three Sons: Human History in Three Dimensions.* Grand Rapids, Mich.: Zondervan Publishing House, 1975.

Davidheiser, Bolton. *Evolution and Christian Faith.* Nutley, N.J.: Presbyterian and Reformed Publishing Company, 1969.

Fair, Wayne and Davis, P. William. *The Case for Creation.* Revised Edition. Chicago: Moody Press, 1972.

Gish, Duane T. *Speculations and Experiments on the Origin of Life.* San Diego: Institute for Creation Research, 1972.

Gish, Duane T. *Evolution, The Fossils Say NO!,* San Diego: Institute for Creation Research, second edition, 1973.

Howe, George F., ed. *Speak to the Earth: Creation Studies in Geoscience.* Nutley, N.J.: Presbyterian and Reformed Publishing Company, 1975.

Klotz, John W. *Genes, Genesis and Evolution.* St. Louis: Concordia Publishing House, 1970.

Lammerts, Walter E., ed. *Why Not Creation?* Nutley, N.J.: Presbyterian and Reformed Publishing Company, 1970.

Lammerts, Walter E., ed. *Scientific Studies in Special Creation.* Nutley, N.J.: Presbyterian and Reformed Publishing Company, 1971.

Macbeth, Norman. *Darwin Retried: An Appeal to Reason.* New York: Dell Publishing Company, Inc., 1973.

Moore, John N. *Questions and Answers on Creation/Evolution.* Grand Rapids, Mich.: Baker Book House, 1976.

Moore, John N. and Slusher, Harold S., eds. *Biology: A Search for Order in Complexity.* Second edition. Grand Rapids, Mich.: Zondervan Publishing House, 1974.

Morris, Henry M. *The Troubled Waters of Evolution.* San Diego: Creation-Life Publishers, 1974.

Morris, Henry M., ed. *Scientific Creationism*. San Diego: Creation-Life Publishers, 1974.

Morris, Henry M. *The Genesis Record*. Grand Rapids, Mich.: Baker Book House, 1976.

Riegle, David D. *Creation or Evolution?* Grand Rapids, Mich.: Zondervan Publishing House, 1971.

Slusher, Harold S. *Critique of Radiometric Dating*. San Diego: Institute for Creation Research, 1973.

Smith, A.E. Wilder. *Man's Origin and Man's Destiny*. Wheaton, Ill.: Harold Shaw Company, 1968.

Smith, A.E. Wilder. *The Creation of Life*. Wheaton, Ill.: Harold Shaw Company, 1970.

Whitcomb, John C., Jr., and Morris, Henry M. *The Genesis Flood*. Philadelphia: Presbyterian and Reformed Publishing Company, 1961.

Whitcomb, John C., Jr. *The Origin of the Solar System*. Nutley, N.J.: Presbyterian and Reformed Publishing Company, 1964.

Whitcomb, John C., Jr. *The Early Earth*. Nutley, N.J.: Craig Press, 1972.

Whitcomb, John C., Jr. *The World That Perished*. Grand Rapids, Mich.: Baker Book House, 1973.

Wysong, R.L. *The Creation-Evolution Controversy*. East Lansing, Mich.: Inquiry Press, 1976.

Zimmerman, Paul A., ed. *Darwin, Evolution and Creation*. St. Louis: Concordia Publishing House, 1959.

Zimmerman, Paul A., ed. *Creation, Evolution, and God's Word*. St. Louis: Concordia Publishing House, 1972.

Recommended Periodicals

Acts and Facts. Monthly. Institute for Creation Research. San Diego, California.

Creation Research Society Quarterly. Creation Research Society, Ann Arbor, Michigan.

Bibliography

Below is a list of articles by Dr. John N. Moore published since he became an active spokesman for creationism. Descriptions of his efforts have appeared in numerous newspaper articles across the United States, plus two feature articles: "The Surprising Professor of Non-Evolution," *Moody Monthly* (December, 1973) and "MSU's Back-to-Genesis Man," *Wonderland Magazine,* The Grand Rapids Press (April 25, 1971). Dr. Moore has also presented numerous papers before state and national scientific research and science teaching associations.

General Articles:
"Another Choice"
Decision Magazine, January, 1975, pp. 3-4.
>   This article was also printed in the Australian and Great Britain Editions, January, 1975, and in the South American Spanish Edition, October, 1975.

"Evolution, Creation, and the Scientific Method"
>   *The American Biology Teacher,* January, 1973, pp. 23-26.

"Teach Creation in School"
>   *Child Evangelism,* Steptember, 1972, pp. 8-10, 33.

Technical Papers:
"Some Definitional Formulations"
>   *Creation Research Society Quarterly,* June, 1974, pp. 3-5.

"Evolution, Creation, Scientific Method, and Legislation"
>   *Michigan Science Teachers Bulletin,* Winter, 1974, pp. 6-14. Winter, 1974.

"Retrieval System Problems with Articles in *Evolution*"
>   *Creation Research Society Quarterly,* September, 1973, pp. 110-117.

"Dialogue: Paleontologic Evidence and Organic Evolution"
>   *Journal of the American Scientific Affiliation,* December, 1972, pp. 160-176. (Co-authored with Professor J. Cuffey, Dept. of Geosciences, The Pennsylvania State University)

"On Chromosomes, Mutations, and Phylogeny"
>   *Creation Research Society Quarterly,* December, 1972, pp. 159-171.

"Comment on the Possible Relation of the Theory of Evolution and the Genesis Account of Creation in a Science Course", *Michigan Science Teachers Bulletin,* October-November, 1972, pp. 26-30.

"On Evolutionists and Their Cloak of Ideas"
Creation Research Society Quarterly, June, 1971, pp. 76-77.

"Should Evolution Be Taught?"
Creation Research Society Quarterly, September, 1970, pp. 105-116.

"Evolution: Required or Optional in a Science Course?"
Journal of the American Scientific Affiliation, September, 1970, pp. 82-87.

"Neo-Darwinism and Society"
Creation Research Society Quarterly, January, 1966, pp. 13-23.

Aspects of Scientific Activity

In chapter 3, "Facts about a Theory," two main kinds of scientific activities were mentioned: empirical and theoretical. On the opposite page a detailed outline of these two subdivisions is presented. It is important to note that proper *scientific* theories involve some imaginary aspect, such as atoms, molecules, or genes; nevertheless, these are at least *indirectly* detectable. All imagined stellar explosions, spontaneous generations of life, movements of masses of dry rock to form mountains and accidental mutational changes that might have resulted in new organs and/or physical traits in living organisms are distinctly *not* detectable. Therefore any "theory" involving such concepts must be considered rigorously as *nonscientific.*

Also of special importance is the itemization of basic assumptions or presuppositions that are the logical "grounds" for *all* scientific work, and in fact, all intellectual endeavor regardless of discipline.

Aspects of Scientific Activity

Observations (including initial observations)—recorded
awarenesses (prior)

Descriptions
   Classification—grouping, ordering
Calculations—numerical manipulations
Problems—questions (?)
Hypotheses—testable
   (tentative ans.)   Analogy   Controlled   Trial
                             Experimentation
              Inductive   and
Generalizations—laws   reasoning   (testing)
                                            Error
Predictions—testable
   (if . . . then)   (Experimental
                              assumptions)
              Deductive
              reasoning

THEORETICAL ←→ EMPIRICAL

Scientific theory (Theoretical model) (Conceptual scheme)
   Theoretical assumptions—imaginary aspect   atom
                          object or event   molecule
                                       gene
     (list of postulates)
     Theorems—deductive reasoning
     (predictions)

Foundational, Basic Assumptions (or Presuppositions)

   a. Objectivity of study
   b. Cause and effect
   c. Testability of ideas
   d. Objects/events independent (outside) of observers
   e. Uniformity of natural environment

Criteria for a Good Scientific Theory

Below, rigorous criteria for identification of a proper scientific theory are provided. These criteria are quoted from an outstanding textbook for physical science.

Qualifications 1 and 3 are very important to any conceptualization of first origins. Very critical is the fact that no "prior observations" are possible, since no man observed first origins of the universe, life, or humankind; nor is it possible to "check with experience by test" in any manner when objective considerations are given to first origins.

Three qualifications have already been cited:

1. A fruitful theory *correlates many separate facts,* particularly the important *prior observations,* in a logical preferably easily grasped structure of thought.
2. In the course of continued use it *suggests new relations* and stimulates directed research.
3. The theory permits us to deduce predictions that *check with experience* by test, and it is useful for clearing up puzzling difficulties and solving practical problems.

The history of science has shown that a good theory frequently has, in addition to the three attributes above, one or more of the following three:

4. When the smoke of initial battle has lifted, the more successful of two rival theories often turns out to be the one that is simpler in the sense that it involves *fewer basic assumptions or hypotheses.*
5. A theory is more readily acceptable to contemporary scientists if its *postulates or assumptions are plausible.*
6. Successful theory is flexible enough to grow, and to *undergo modifications* where necessary.

—From Chapter 8, "On the Nature of Scientific Theory," in *Foundations of Modern Physical Science* by Gerald Holton and Duane H.D. Holler. Reading, Mass.: Addison-Wesley Publishing Company, Inc., 1958.

Examples of Good Scientific Theories

On the basis of the previous list of criteria for discerning a proper theory, is the so-called theory of evolution scientific? No. In no way are any prior observations of the first stages of the universe, of first life, or the first humankind possible.

Then what are good examples of scientific theories? On this page postulates of four outstanding examples of sound scientific theories are listed. Though some imaginary aspect is involved in each of these scientific theories, multiple tests by experience, though accomplished through indirect means, can be repeated over and over again with regard to atoms, molecules, and genes.

Postulates of Gene Theory
1. Genes exist in pairs per trait, usually, in zygotes, body cells, and gonadal generative cells.
2. Only one gene per trait, usually, exists in gametes.
3. Two genes exist per trait, usually, in a zygote after fertilization.
4. One gene may be dominant to another gene.
5. Gene pairs may combine randomly and independently during gamete formation and as a result of fertilization.
6. A series of genes may influence the same trait.
7. More than one gene are located on a single chromosome.
8. Exchange of genes is possible, as exchange of chromosome parts occurs.
9. More than one pair of genes may influence the same trait.

Postulates of Gas Kinetic Theory
1. All matter is composed of small particles.
2. Gas molecules are small compared with distance between them.

3. Particles are in motion.
4. When molecules collide with each other or walls of a container there is no loss of energy.
5. The average kinetic energy of all different gas molecules is the same at the same temperature.
6. The energy of molecular motion is heat energy, that is, the temperature of a gas is a measure of the average kinetic energy of the molecules.

Postulates of Dalton's Atomic Theory (Nineteenth Century)
1. All matter is composed of ultimate particles, called atoms, which are indivisible.
2. All the particles of a given element are alike in weight and in all other aspects. (But particles of different elements have different weights.)
3. Atoms are indestructible by chemical means and their identities are not changed in all chemical reactions.
4. Chemical combination occurs by the union of the atoms of the elements in simple numerical ratios.

Postulates of Nuclear-electron Theory
1. Atom is composed of nucleus surrounded by a cloud of electrons.
2. Nucleus is composed of protons and neutrons.
3. Proton is a positive charge.
4. Electron has a negative charge.
5. Number of protons equals number of electrons.
6. The number of positive charges on the nucleus is called the atomic number.
7. Neutrons are uncharged particles which still have mass.
8. Atomic weight of an element is the sum of the number of protons and neutrons in the nucleus.
9. Atoms of an element may have the same atomic number but different atomic weights (isotopes).

Different Patterns of Thought

The abstract on these pages adds another dimension to the importance of sound scientific activities. No man as a scientist can speak authoritatively about first origins of the universe, life, or humankind. No man as a scientist has made any prior observations, nor is he able to conduct tests by experience of any such events.

However, men have had ideas about first origins, beside the ever-constant, unchanging answers about first origins in the Holy

---

Three Phases of Mental Procedure

Method of the Ruling Theory**		Method of the Working Hypothesis
1 Habit of precipitative explanation	Scientific study be-gan with simple determining of facts. Reformation demanded statistical instead of causal. Vitality of study quickly disappears when the mere collection of unmeaning facts is the sole objective.	1 A means of determining facts rather than a proposition to be established
2 Interpretation precedes serious inquiry		2 Function is the suggestion and guidance of lines of inquiry
3 Application of theory to like phenomenon leads mind into the delusion that the theory has been strengthened by additional facts		3 Hypothesis is a means, not an end in itself
4 Intellectual affection takes hold and leads to unreserved adoption of the theory: a special searching for phenomena that support the theory		4 Care must be taken to prevent the working hypothesis from becoming a controlling idea
5 Biasing tendencies		5 Historical antecedents lend a good influence toward preservation of integrity of working hypothesis.
6 Tentative theory → and adopted theory → a ruling theory		

**"I use the term 'theory' here instead of hypothesis because the latter associated with a better-controlled and more circumspect habit of mir This restrained habit leads to the use of the less assertive term 'hypothes

Bible. Various "ruling theories" have been popular. Today the neo-Darwinian, modern synthetic evolutionary viewpoint, is the dominant and ruling position taken by the majority of men. Notice the different patterns of thought characteristic of the Ruling Theory, Working Hypothesis, and Multiple Working Hypotheses, as condensed from an important article by a prominent nineteenth-century geologist.

Method of Multiple Working Hypotheses

To protect against the defects of the other methods, multiple working hypotheses distribute efforts and divide effections toward ideas.

1 Effort is to bring into view every rational explanation of the phenomenon and to develop every tenable hypothesis relative to its nature, cause, or origin

2 Investigator becomes the parent of a family of hypotheses; therefore counter-action of the chief danger that springs from affection is effected

3 With neutralized partialities of his emotional nature, the investigator is able to enforce a mental attitude in the inquiry which allows for some of his hypotheses to perish

4 The method allows for success of several hypotheses which is in line with recognition of coordination of the several causes of phenomena

5 Use of a full staff of rational hypotheses coordinately invites thoroughness, equipoise, and symmetry

6 The method allows the reaction of one hypothesis upon another which tends to amplify the recognized scope of each: "The keenness of the analytic process advocates the closeness of differentiating criteria, and the sharpness of discrimination is promoted by the coordinate working of several competitive hypotheses"

7 Develops "the habit of parallel thought" or "of complex thought"; encourages the viewing of phenomena analytically and synthetically at the same time

An Abstract of "The Method of Multiple Working Hypotheses" by T. C. Chamberlin, *Journal of Geology*, Vol. 39: pp. 155-165, 1931 (Reprint of *Journal of Geology*, Vol. 5: pp. 837-848, 1897)

ile the mind in the habit here sketched more often believes itself to have ached the higher ground of a theory and more often employs the term eory'" (p. 157).

Outlines of Two Foundational Models of Origins

There are just two foundational viewpoints regarding first origins: the evolution (or evolutionary uniformitarianism) model, and the creation (or catastrophism and creationism) model. The first is a viewpoint or world-view generated by those with prior commitments to the philosophy of naturalism; the second is a viewpoint or world-view generated by those with prior commitments to the philosophy of theism.

In very brief and condensed form the primary points held by proponents of the two foundational viewpoints of models regarding first origins have been formulated in the two columns of the following chart.

Statements of Evolutionary Uniformitarianism	Statements of Catastrophism and Creationism
Model of Origins	**Model of Origins**
(based upon world-view of naturalism)	(based upon world-view of theism)

1. Matter has existed eternally (no cause).
  a. Matter continually appears (from energy?).
  b. Matter exploded and continues to expand.
	1. Universe was created essentially in present state. (Cause: eternal Creator)
	  a. Matter, planets, stars created complete.
	  b. Light rays created directly.

2. A whole series of elements was generated (evolved); and stars, planets have evolved by accretion.	2. Universe was created complete and basically stable.
3. Apparent land features resulted from specific causes of vulcanism, diastrophism, gradation (the present is the key to the past).	3. Causes seen in present were not causes of land features (the present is only the key to the present).
4. Forces of origination and integration exist.	4. Catastrophism, decay, and conservational activities prevail in antagonism.

Statements of Evolutionary Uniformitarianism	Statements of Catastrophism and Creationism
Model of Origins	**Model of Origins**
5. Geologic column is evidence of vast "history" of the earth.	5. Only local sedimentary columns exist and world-wide destruction is evidenced by world-wide distribution of sedimentary rocks.
6. Because of innate propensity of matter, organic matter came from inorganic matter by spontaneous generation.	6. Since spontaneous generation of life is contradictory to Second Law of Thermodynamics, only special creation of life could be cause of life.
7. Changes in evolutionary sequence of life forms are due to random mutational changes in genes.	7. Mutations are evidence of increased disorder (entropy) and only changes *within* limits of kinds, group, or species result from mutations/recombination of genes.
8. Changes of complex forms or kinds from less complex kinds are the result of accumulation of random variations.	8. Conservative processes are involved in operation of genetic code resulting in essential stability (fixity) of basic kinds, groups, species, with no accumulation of random variations.
9. Mankind is related to the ape through an unknown common ancestor.	9. Mankind is a special creation.
10. Fossils of genus *Homo* are immediate ancestors of modern man.	10. "Ape-like" features of prehistoric man may be due to disease and degeneration.
11. Races of man resulted from mutations and segregation in early man-like forms.	11. Human beings all belong to one race and languages are merely tribal differences.
12. Evolutionary humanism can be a guiding faith.	12. Alienation, identity, and relevance can be answered in context of relation to Creator God.

About "Theistic Evolution"

A third explanation about possible first origins seems attractive to many persons: God could have used evolution as a means to bring about the tremendous diversity of celestial objects and variety of life on this earth. This idea is commonly called "theistic evolution." And a quick reading of Genesis 1 may impress one that that sequence may be comparable to the ancestry of living organisms adopted by evolutionists. But the comparison is *only superficial,* as may be seen by close study and examination of the chart on the next page.

If significant correlation existed between Genesis 1 and "mega-evolution" then a great number of horizontal lines would be evident between entries in the two columns of the chart. Clearly no significant correlation exists as is manifest by the confusing network of broken lines.

Is the Order of Appearance Comparable?

Evolution (Mega-evolution)	Revelation (Genesis of Life)
Placental mammals and early man	Man (male and female)
Marsupial mammals, angiosperms	
Dinosaurs, birds, egg-laying mammals	
Mammal-like reptiles	Living creature (land), cattle, creeping things, beasts of the earth
Reptiles, fern-like plants, gymnosperms	Moving creature, fowl, great whale (fish), every living creature (water) that moveth
Amphibians, vascular plants	
Insects	Greater light (sun), lesser light (moon), stars
Fishes, some land plants	
Primitive vertebrates and proto-chodates	Grass, herb yielding seed, fruit tree yielding fruit
Some algae, fungi, modern invertebrates	
	Light
Galaxies, stars, planets	Heaven and earth
Explosion of dense particle	
Eternal matter	Eternal Creator (Jesus Christ)

IS THERE ANY SIGNIFICANT CORRELATION?

Ideas on the Origin of Life

What are the basic nuclei of thoughts of the five themes found in men's writings over the centuries with respect to the origin of life? On the next page pro and con aspects of these five themes have been reduced to specific and explicit expressions.

For ease in identifying the time periods of each of the first three themes, names of major proponents and/or experimenters have been included parenthetically. Actually the last two themes listed have been included in men's thinking almost as long as any recorded attention to the question about first origins of life.

PRO-Position

↑ ABIOGENESIS ↓

1. Macrozoic ideas:
   Ancient people *believed* in spontaneous generation of *whole* organisms, because they thought they saw mice come from mud and snakes from horses' hair, etc. (Aristotle, others)
2. Microzoic ideas:
   Next people *believed* in spontaneous generation of microbes or bacteria because Pouchet (1860) and others thought they saw such occur in nutrient broths.
3. Sub-microzoic ideas:
   Today many scientists *believe* in spontaneous generation of subvital units of matter that formed into "coacervates" or "proteinoids." (Darwin believed in one or many beginnings; Oparin be-

CON-Position

↑ BIOGENESIS ↓

1. Conclusive controlled experimentation of Francisco Redi (1650) with covered and uncovered meat *established* "life came from life," at least flies from maggots which came from eggs.
2. Conclusive work by Appert and controlled experimentation by Louis Pasteur (1864) with swan-necked flasks *established* that bacteria may be dust-laden and a source of bacterial life from life.
3. Instantaneous synthesis of amino acids requires human intervention, hence no man can study spontaneous generation, which by definition entails *no external* intervention. (Blum, Cook point out

102

PRO-Position	CON-Position

ABIOGENESIS (left column, vertical label)
BIOGENESIS (right column, vertical label)

lieved in one combination of subvital units; Miller, Fox, Pannapurumma have used controlled experimentation to *synthesize* amino acids, which are not living.)

4. Cosmozoic ideas:
Over the decades and still today some scientists *believe* that life came to the earth from other planets or other parts of the universe by way of "spores" or meteorites.

5. Theozoic ideas:
Over the centuries some scientists *believe* life is a result of supernatural creative acts of Creator God; life that has always been complex.
(Note: Beliefs in #1 thru #4 all entail supranatural events.)

---

chance of life coming from no life; Coppedge indicates high improbability of *only left*-handed protein substances in living organisms.)

4. These ideas "beg the question", side-step problem of origin of life; no other planets known from space probes (Mercury, Venus, Mars, Jupiter, or Saturn[?]) seem to have life as we know it. Heat of meteorites, X rays, ultraviolet light would have real deleterious effects on life.

5. No scientific study possible, but a Creator of life would not be in contradiction to concepts of cause and effect, or degradation or degeneration from complex organizational order.

What Are the Choices?

The following quotations are provided to clarify the point that reputable scientists in the last two centuries have expressed themselves in clearly written form that there are only three possible choices as to the origin of life.

A. *One spontaneous coming together of inorganic matter to form living substance from which all other forms and stages of life have come.*

"If life comes only from life, does this mean that there was *always* life on the earth? It must, yet we know that this cannot be so. We know that the world was once without life—that life appeared later. How? We think it was by spontaneous generation " (*Biological Science: An Inquiry into Life* [Harcourt, Brace & World, Inc., 1963], p. 42.)

"The important point is that since the origin of life belongs in the category of at-least-once phenomena, time is on its side. However improbable we regard this event, . . . given enough time it will almost certainly happen at least once. . . . Time is in fact the hero of the plot. The time with which we have to deal is on the order of two billion years. What we regard as impossible on the basis of human experience is meaningless here. Given so much time, the 'impossible' becomes possible, the possible probable, and the probable virtually certain. One has only to wait: time itself performs miracles " (George Wald, "The Origin of Life," in *The Physics and Chemistry of Life* [Simon & Shuster, 1955], p. 12).

B. *Multiple coming together of inorganic matter to form living substance from which* all *life forms have come along separate* lines.

"Multiple biopoeses have been proposed most boldly by R. L. Berg (1959). Similar is the proposal of repetitive neobiogenesis of Keosin (1960) " (J. R. Nursall, "On the Origins of the Major Groups of Animals " [*Evolution,* 16; 1962], p. 118).

"The difficulty of placing viruses, bacteria, certain 'algae,' sponges, and so on, in a fitting scheme based on a monophyletic hypothesis may stem from the possibility that the discontinuities are real and represent the existence of separate lines of descent from independent instances of neobiogenesis at different times in the history of the earth down to the present " (John Keosin, [*Science* 131, February 19, 1960], p. 482). "The word neobiogenesis is employed here to describe the repeated origination of life in nature ever since life began " (John Keosin, *The Origin of Life* [Reinhold, 1964], p. 98).

C. *Special creation of basic life forms or kinds originating from an Almighty Being and* all *life forms known coming as variants* within *limits of original kinds.*

". . . 'Creation,' in the ordinary sense of the word, is perfectly conceivable. I find no difficulty in conceiving that, at some former period, this universe was not in existence; and that it made its appearance in six days (or instantaneously, if that is preferred), in consequence of the volition of some preexisting Being. Then, as now, the so-called *a priori* arguments against Theism, and, given a Deity, against the possibility of creative acts, appeared to me to be devoid of reasonable foundation" (Leonard Huxley, editor. *Life and Letters of Thomas Henry Huxley,* Vol. II. [Macmillan, 1903], p. 429).
"If so, it will present a parallel to the theory of evolution itself, a theory universally accepted not because it can be proved by logically coherent evidence to be true but because the only alternative, special creation, is clearly incredible " (D.M.S. Watson. "Adaptation," *Nature* 124, 1929, p. 233.)

On the Fixity of Species

The concept of "fixity of species" has perennially been used by non-creationist thinkers to try to discredit creationism. It is true that early creationist biologists such as Carl Linnaeus and John Ray once thought God had created directly every species of organism which they had identified.

However, many modern scientists, and especially those with prior commitments to evolutionism, are apparently unaware that Linnaeus, at least, changed his mind after years of specific research in plant hybridization. Documentation that Linnaeus changed his mind is reproduced on the next page.

It is true that Linnaeus wrote in 1735 in his *Classes Plantarum:*

> There are as many species as there are
> originally created forms.

From this point of view he did most of his work in classification.

However, it is interesting to note what he wrote in his book *Systema Vegetabilium* (1774), written four years before his death. During the later years of his life he carried on considerable hybridization of his own and as a result came to broaden definitely his concept of the created unit.

In the book *Stages in the Evolution of Plant Species* (Cornell University Press, 1951, pp. 4-5), Jen Clausen translated from the Latin the following assertion made by Linnaeus in his 1774 book:

> Let us suppose that the Divine Being in the beginning progressed from the simpler to the complex; from few to many; similarly that He in the beginning of the plant kingdom created as many plants as there were natural orders. These plant orders He himself, therefrom producing, mixed among themselves until from them originated those plants which today exist as genera.
>
> Nature then mixed up these plant genera among themselves through generations of double origin [=hybrids] and multiplied them into the existing species, as many as possible (whereby the flower structures were not changed), excluding from the number of species the almost sterile hybrids, which are produced by the same mode of origin.

106

Crosses between Kinds

That the biblical phrases "after his kind" and "after their kind" might very well be equated with the modern creationist phrase "fixity of kinds" is a plausible deduction from data provided on the next page.

Crosses between horse and donkey to produce a mule, between zebra and horse to produce a zeedunk (or zebronkey), and between lion and tiger to produce a liger or tigon were mentioned in chapter 7, "Option for a Scientist." Nevertheless, hybrids from such crosses are invariably sterile and do not reproduce and hence *no new kind* is produced. Man's intervention is required to obtain most crosses listed on these two pages. The quotation from Dr. Frank L. Marsh is excellent empirical support for "fixity of kinds."

NOTE: Evolutionists are anxious to have people accept "transitional forms" between major kinds of organisms; i.e., between amphibians and reptiles, between reptiles and birds, etc. They regularly point to *Archaeopteryx* as a fossil bird that could have been a transitional form. Nevertheless ornithologists clearly claim *Archaeopteryx* as a *bird*. Furthermore, no trace of half-legs or half-wings or any other nascent organ can be found among any fossil remains. Absolutely no demonstrable transitional forms exist in the fossil record.

A Working List of Crosses
Based on Authentic Records

A. Crossing has taken place at least to the extent of beginning of embryonic development between the following more common animals:

1. lion x tiger
2. mouse x rat
3. sheep x goat
4. chicken x guinea fowl
5. chicken x turkey
6. house martin x barn swallow
7. swan x goose
8. horse, ass, zebra, kiang x onager
9. dogs, wolves, jackals, coyotes x some foxes
10. ox, zebu, yak, bison, wisent, Brahman cattle x Afrikander cattle

B. Hybrids are frequent across gaps which may not appear so wide:

1. among "species" of ducks
2. among "species" of pheasants
3. among "species" of crows
4. among "species" of pigeons
5. among "species" of Cecropia moth
6. among "species" of toads
7. among "species" of coyotes
8. among rabbits and hares
9. among "species" of ibex
10. among "species of caribou
11. among purple and bronzed grackles
12. between red-shafted and yellow-shafted flickers
13. between western and eastern "species" of the European hedgehog
14. between English sparrow and willow sparrow
15. between some "species" of warblers
16. between some "species" of gall wasps
17. between some "species" of fresh-water fish

C. Among plants some of the widest crosses known are those of:

1. wheat x wheat grass
2. goat grass x rye
3. corn x teosinte and gama grass
4. radish x cabbage
5. sugar cane x sorghum
6. fescue grass x Italian rye grass
7. wild tobacco x petunia
8. bean x cow pea
9. blackberry x raspberry

D. Actually "species" within the following plant "genera" will cross with other "species" of the same "genera" and produce hybrids:

1. Alder	26. Honey locust
2. Arbutus	27. Larch
3. Basswood	28. Lily
4. Birch	29. Black Locust
5. Buckeye	30. Magnolia
6. Canna	31. Maple
7. Carnation	32. Oak
8. Catalpa	33. Oats
9. Catchfly	34. Onion
10. Chestnut	35. Papaw
11. Cotton	36. Pea
12. Currant	37. Pine
13. Darnel	38. Poplar
14. Dogwood	39. Poppy
15. Elm	40. Rose
16. Evening primrose	41. Snapdragon
17. Fir	42. Spiderwort
18. Four-o'clock	43. Spruce
19. Goat grass	44. Sycamore
20. Gooseberry	45. Timothy grass
21. Hawk's-beard	46. Tobacco
22. Hawthorne	47. Vetch
23. Hemlock	48. Wheat
24. Hickory	49. Willow
25. Holly	50. Yew

NOTE: " 'Lemon-lime' plants have been reported as a successful hybrid of the two citrus fruits with the 'greater qualities of both parents' " (*Lansing State Journal,* Oct. 29, 1972, p. F-8).
Hybridization is important as a means of production of variation among plants and animals, but *no* crosses occur across kinds; hence diversity *within* the kind is all that is accomplished.

—from *Evolution, Creation and Science* by Frank Lewis Marsh, Ph.D., Review and Herald Publishing Association, 1947, pp. 157ff.

Chromosome Counts in Animals and Plants

Another type of sound scientific evidence, gained through the practice of multiple, repeated observations, is presented in two charts below. After careful check of commonly used biology textbooks, Dr. Moore has yet to find any chart as thorough as those provided on these pages.

The pattern of placement of various typical categories of animals and plants used by modern taxonomists and systematists is drawn up to coincide with the popularly accepted (or "revealed consensus," as some writers mention) ancestry of organism groups, according to the neo-Darwinian, modern synthetic evolutionary viewpoint.

If there was any increase of complexity in organisms from so-called simple forms of life, then one might reasonably expect that such an increase would be reflected in increase in numbers of chromosomes by means of which DNA genic material is commonly transferred from generation to generation among sexually reproducing organisms. Clearly no pattern of increase of chromosome number is evident in these two charts.

NOTE: Ever since the invention of the electron microscope, no one can validly refer to "simple" life. *All cells are complex,* and apparently always have been complex. Hence the minimum claim by evolutionists would be that life supposedly changed from "least complex" to "most complex" according to their imagined schema.

CHROMOSOME COUNT IN ANIMALS
(2n only)

AVES:

Rhea 42-68
Passer 40-48, 54-60
Meopstittacus 50-60
Callus 12-44

Anas 43-49, 80
Columba 50, 31-62
Larus 60

REPTILIA:

Elaphe 36
Hemidactylus 46
Alligator 32
Chamaeleon 24

Laceria 36, 38
Emys 50
Anguis 36, 44

AMPHIBIA:

Rana, 16, 24, 26, 39
Salamandra 24
Cryptobranchus 56, 62

Bufo 22
Triton 18-24

MAMMALIA:

Ornithorhynchus 70
Didelphys 17-22
Erinaceus 48
Sorex 23
Lepus 36-46
Peromyscus 48, 52
Microtus 42, 46, 50
Apodemus 46, 48, 50
Mus 40, 44
Rattus 46, 62

Canis 50, 64, 78
Felis 35, 38
Bos 16, 20, 60
Capra 60
Ovis 33, 48, 54, 60
Sus 18, 38, 40
Equus 60, 66
Rhesus 42, 48
Homo 46

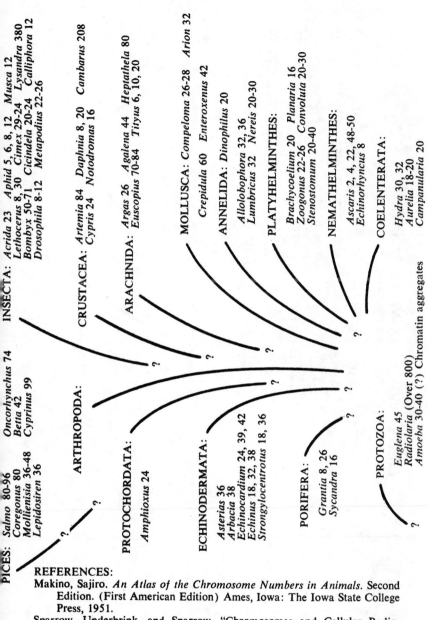

REFERENCES:

Makino, Sajiro. *An Atlas of the Chromosome Numbers in Animals.* Second Edition. (First American Edition) Ames, Iowa: The Iowa State College Press, 1951.

Sparrow, Underbrink, and Sparrow. "Chromosomes and Cellular Radio-sensitivity," *Radiation Research*, Vol. 32:915-945, 1967.

CHROMOSOME COUNT IN PLANTS
(2n, except as indicated)

ANGIOSPERMS:

GYMNOSPERMS:

Abies 24
Cupressus 22
Cycas 22
Gingko 24
Juniperus 22-24, 44
Picea 24
Pinus 24
Larix 24
Taxus 24
Thuja 22
Tsuga 24
Sequoia 66
Zamia 16, 18

MONOCOTYLEDONS:

Allium 16, 20, 56
Amaryllis 22
Crocus 6, 8, 10, 20, 26
Canna 18, 36
Carex 106
Elodea 16, 24, 48
Iris 32, 42
Lilium 24
Narcissus 14, 26, 28
Poa 14, 28, 42, 56, 63, 70, 147
Smilax 32, 60
Sorghum 10, 20, 40
Tradescantia 12, 18, 24
Triticum 14, 28, 42
Vallisneria 20, 40
Yucca 60

DICOTYLEDONS:

Brassica 18, 20
Chrysanthemum 18, 36, 56, 138, 198
Clematis 16
Helianthus 34
Phaseolus 22
Primula 16, 22, 36
Ranunculus 16, 32, 48
Rumex 20, 40, 60
Salix 40, 63
Sedum 20, 44, 54, 68
Petunia 14
Raphanus 16, 18, 20, 38

PTERIDOPHYTES:

Adiantum 60, 120, 116
Diphasium 46
Diplazium 82, 123
Dryopteris 82, 123
Elaphoglossum 82
Isoetes 33, 44
Ophioglossum 960, 1100
Polypodium 72, 111, 148
Polystichum 82, 164
Psilotum 208
Lycopodium 46, 340, 528
Pteris 58, 76, 87, 115
Selaginella 20, 36
Thelypteris (n=29, 36, 62, 72)

MOSS:

Anthoceros (n=6)
Arctoa (n=14)
Bazzania (n=9)
Claopodium (n=11)
Haplohymenium (n=11)
Jungermannia (n=9)
Marchantia 9
Porella (n=8)
Radula (n=8)

?

?

SEED FERNS

112

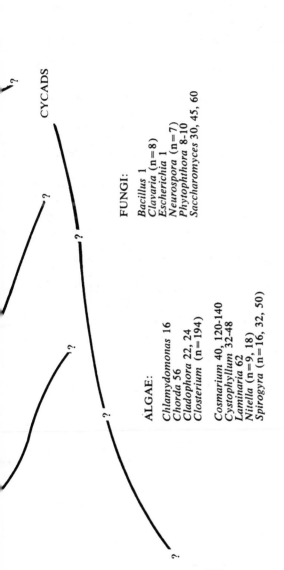

CYCADS

FUNGI:

Bacillus 1
Clavaria (n=8)
Escherichia 1
Neurospora (n=7)
Phytophthora 8-10
Saccharomyces 30, 45, 60

ALGAE:

Chlamydomonas 16
Chorda 56
Cladophora 22, 24
Closterium (n=194)

Cosmarium 40, 120-140
Cystophyllum 32-48
Laminaria 62
Nitella (n=9, 18)
Spirogyra (n=16, 32, 50)

REFERENCES:

Ornduff, R. Editor. *Index to Plant Chromosome Numbers for 1965.* Utrecht, Netherlands: International Bureau for Plant Taxonomy and Nomenclature of the International Association for Plant Taxonomy, June, 1967.

Ornduff, R. Editor. *Index to Plant Chromosome Numbers for 1966.* Utrecht, Netherlands: International Bureau for Plant Taxonomy and Nomenclature of the International Association for Plant Taxonomy, June, 1968.

Darlington, C. D. and A. P. Wylie. *Chromosome Atlas of Flowering Plants.* Second Edition, London: George Allen and Unwin Ltd., 1955.

113

Imagined Explanation in "Historical" Geology

Manifestly characteristic of the scenario writing or imaginative narratives featured in writings of "historical" geologists is the "history" of the Grand Canyon in the southwestern United States, which is represented diagrammatically on the next page. Supposedly the huge region surrounding the Grand Canyon was inundated by water of various "seas" and/or shallow water overflows six or more times. And this total does not include two other series of sedimentation (which "historical" geologists claim resulted from accumulation of rock debris and sediments *under water*), usually named the Ordovician and Silurian Periods. Rocks usually assigned to these two periods of time of the popularly accepted geologic time scale have presumably been completely eroded away, since no evidence can be found of Ordovician or Silurian rocks in the Grand Canyon layers.

Men who believe that such changes of the earth's surface actually occurred do so solely as a result of their carefully designed "reconstructions." Formation of the Grand Canyon as a result of degradation and erosion of still soft sedimentary layers after the world-wide Noachian flood entails a much more economical position. Imagination of the *fewest* causes and effects to "explain" present conditions is usually preferred by scientists. Not so, evidently, where water flooding is concerned.

Imagined Explanation

Code	Geol. Era	Geol. Period	Age (millions)	"Historical" Events
O	P A L E O Z O I C		245	Erosion _____ Uplift
N		Permian		_____ Deeper Water
M				Deposition
L			275	Shallow water (swamp)
K		Pennsylvanian	310	Shallow water Uplift
J		Mississippian	350	Erosion Uplift / Sea water
I		Devonian	365-400	Erosion Uplift / Sea Water — Silurian / Ordovician
H		Cambrian		Erosion Uplift
G				
F			510-540	Deposition Missing
E	P R O T E R O Z O I C			Erosion
D				
C				Faulting
B			500-1000	Deposition
A	Archeo-zoic		2000	Erosion / Metamorphosed / Deposition

- - - GRAND CANYON - - -

115

On "Living Fossils"

The combination of the terms *living* and *fossils* seems incongruous and contradictory. Actually, all the organisms mentioned on these two pages were once considered extinct. Interestingly enough, viable, definitely alive specimens of both supposedly extinct animals and plants have been found since 1900.

Certainly the types, forms, or kinds of animals and plants associated (or classified) with these "living fossils" have continued on the earth for extremely long periods of time, if the popularly accepted geologic time scale is correct (which many creationist scientists challenge today, as do even some evolutionary-minded scientists). Such "living fossils" may reasonably be looked upon as excellent empirical evidence for "fixity of kinds," which modern creationist scientists maintain is equivalent to the biblical phrases "after his kind" and "after their kind."

The following plants and animals were supposed to have been extinct for at least several millions of years, but they have been found alive and thriving somewhere in the world.

1. Crinoids: Flower-like echinoderms, commonly called sea lilies or feather stars. There are about 2,100 species of fossil crinoids, and about 800 species of living representatives. Found in Paleozoic strata.

2. Lingula: Within the phylum Brachiopoa, the genus *Lingula* is found attached by a peduncle to the bottom of the oceans in sand or mud. This same genus is found in the fossil marine fauna of the Cambrian strata.

3. Tuatara: This relic is the only survivor of the order Rhynochocephalia, or beak-headed reptiles. Living specimens have been found only on islands off New Zealand, where they live in holes on sandy hills by the shore. The skeleton of one of these reptiles found in Jurassic deposits of Europe is almost exactly like the living tuatara. Fossil evidence of this organism is found in the Early Cretaceous, which supposedly leaves a time gap of 135 million years.

116

4. Coelacanth: In 1937 a coelacanth was caught alive east of London, Cape Province, South Africa. According to the paleontological record, the last coelacanth lived approximately 70 million years ago. More specimens have been taken near Madagascar and the South Africa vicinity. "The bony structures of our modern Coelacanths are almost exactly the same as those left by Coelacanths hundreds of millions of years ago " (J.L.B. Smith, *The Search Beneath the Sea,* Henry Holt and Co., New York, 1956).

5. Neopilina: On May 6, 1952, ten specimens of this deep-sea mollusk were dredged from a depth of 3,590 meters off the Mexican Coast. According to paleontologists, *Neopilina* became extinct about 280 million years ago during the Devonian period. It is not found in intervening rocks.

6. Cycads: *Zamia* grows in parts of Florida, the West Indies, and South America. The East Indian genus *Cycas* attains height of 67 feet and 40 inches in diameter. Fossil cycads, quite abundant in Mesozoic formations, have been found in many areas with abundant remains in the Black Hills region of South Dakota.

7. Metasequoia: Fossils of *Metasequoia* make it the most abundant genus of the Taxodiaceae, or cypress-like family, in North America in the Upper Cretaceous to Miocene formations. Ever since 1946 many living specimens of *Metasequoia* have been found in China. (Chaney, Ralph W., "A Revision of Fossils *Sequoia* and *Taxodium* in Western North America Based on the Recent Discovery of Metasequoia," *Transactions of American Philosophical Society* [1951], pp. 171-263.)

See also: Henry N. Andrews, *Studies in Paleobotany,* (New York: John Wiley and Sons, 1961); Charles M. Bogert, "The Tuatara: Why Is It a Lone Survivor?" *The Scientific Monthly* 76 (1953), pp. 163-170; Maurice-Burton, *Living Fossils* (London: Thames and Hudson, 1954); M. Merrill, E.D. "A Living *Metasequoia* in China", *Science* 170 (1948), p. 140; and A.C. Steward, *Fossil Plants* Vol. IV, (New York: Hafner Publishing Co. 1963).

Identities or Axioms

Mathematicians since Euclid have used axioms and/or identities to represent "given" information; i.e., self-evident concepts or generalizations from which they then deduce further mathmetical relationships.

On these two pages, "Identities or Axioms" regarding aspects of first origins and different terms used by evolutionists are presented as further clarification of such terms.

Identities or Axioms

STUDY OF ORIGIN OF FIRST LIFE **∵** BEYOND { LIMITS OF MAN'S APPLICATION OF CAUSE AND EFFECT (I. E., TESTING)

MODERN IDEAS OF ORIGIN OF LIFE ≡ SPONTANEOUS GENERATION (HETEROGENESIS) AT SUB-MICROSCOPIC LEVEL

ANY LABORATORY "PRODUCTION" OF LIVING SUBSTANCE ≡ SYNTHESIS OF LIVING FROM NON-LIVING ACCORDING TO KNOWN FORMULAE AND **NOT** ACCIDENTAL (NOR ANY CHANCE COMBINATION)

EVOLUTION≢DEVELOPMENT

MICROEVOLUTION ≡ GENETIC VARIATION WITHIN LIMITS OF KIND

Identities or Axioms

MEGAEVOLUTION
(SOMETIMES MACROEVOLUTION)
OR
TRANSMUTATION OF KINDS

$=$

TREE OF LIFE
OVER
GEOLOGIC TIME

KINDS $=$ TYPES $=$ FORMS $\neq$ SPECIES

THEORY OF
ORGANIC EVOLUTION
[ENDS]

$\neq$

THEORY OF
NATURAL SELECTION
WITHIN LIMITS OF KIND
[MEANS]

ORGANIC EVOLUTION
(TRANSMUTATION
OF KINDS)

$\neq$

ANY
GENETIC
CHANGE

Dual Uses of Specific Groups of Scientific Data

Most specialists writing about first origins of life according to so-called organic evolution group data under seven main headings as seen in the chart on the next page.

Here it is shown that the *same data* are used by evolutionist scientists and creationist scientists. Singular emphasis of the proponents of each of these models are denoted by the words *over* the two columns: evolutionists emphasize *similarities;* creationists emphasize *differences.*

Entries opposite each data category should provide the reader with abbreviated indications of how the respective groups of scientists view data.

Since evolutionists use these data to support the idea of common ancestry, which they cannot reproduce or demonstrate, their claims regarding relationship of organism groups are based purely upon circumstances of similarities over which they have no control.

On the other hand, creationists use the *same data* to support their contentions that there are *no connections between kinds* regarding relationship of organism groups. *These contentions are conclusive,* since findings of "no connection" can be reproduced and demonstrated repeatedly. Hence creationists follow positively the criterion of repeatability so important in sound scientific work.

Creationists, therefore, are able to demonstrate conclusive scientific support for their contentions that the biblical phrase "after his kind" and "after their kind" are scientifically confirmable. In contrast, evolutionists base their entire case upon circumstances which limit them scientifically to showing that similarities do exist, but they are totally unable to explain how such similarities came into existence.

Classes of Scientific Data	Emphasizes similarities	Emphasizes differences
	Summary of ways scientific data are used to support Evolution Uniform Model	Summary of ways scientific data are used to support Catastrophic Creation Model
1. Genetics and Variation	Imagined broad change: kind from kind; across kind.	Known limited change: only variation *within* kind.
	Differences due to recombinations and beneficial mutations that have accumulated; slow change	Mutations mostly harmful; result in no new traits; definite breeding gaps; *no connections betweens kinds.*
2. Classification	Similarities are basis of grouping; due to supposed common gene pool of similar genes; supposed "history" of kinds.	Fixity of kinds; *no connections between distinct groups* as due to persistence of basic characteristics due to varieties from different beginnings.
3. Comparative Form of Anatomy	The degree of similarity is basic for degree of relationship; common gene pool, supposed common ancestry	*No real connection of kinds;* similarities could be due to common plan by Creator God; consistence of master plan pressed.
4. Comparative Embryology	Similarity of structure is result of genetic relationship, supposed common gene pool, supposed common ancestry.	*No real connection of kinds;* similarities could be due to common plan by Creator God; consistency of master plan pressed.
5. Geographic Distribution	Supposed descent with change due to modified environments	Barriers, breeding resulted in centers of population growth; *no new kinds;* continental drift idea could be relevant
6. Fossil Evidences	Presumably successive layers provide evidence of succession of life forms; so-called "actual history" of related organism groups.	Definite gaps between kinds, *no intermediate forms;* no real geological column; world-wide flood possible cause; n.b. living fossils = fixity of kinds.
7. Dating Estimates	Data *interpreted* to mean long ages based on certain assumptions of constant decay rate, no contamination. Use radiometric, non-radiometric estimates plus geologic column.	Radiometric dating *assumptions are erroneous;* evidences of young earth noted; rapid burial, likely; catastrophism.

Explanations and Simplicity

By now the reader should be prepared to study a diagrammatic representation of the two fundamental models of origins of animal and plant life. Using the only sound physical evidence that involves more than "appearance," Dr. Moore has drawn attention to gaps in the fossil and plant and animal breeding records.

Often some will propose that belief in one spontaneous generation of life is more simple than belief in multiple creative acts of an omnipotent God. But, Dr. Moore has simply pointed out that modern evolutionism entails multiple upon multiple occasions of fortunate, fortuitous, accidental mutations (DNA errors) whereby supposedly new physical traits have come into existence. Some of these are: (1) cellular life from non-cellular matter; (2) multi-cellular organization from uni-cellular organization; (3) external skeletal forms from non-skeletal forms; (4) insect flight from non-flight condition; (5) vertebrates from nonvertebrates; (6) land animals from aquatic animals; (7) bird flight from nonflight condition; and (8) human consciousness from animal consciousness. Further mention could be made of similar "ideational gaposis" such as land plants from aquatic plants, seed plants from nonseed plants.

Hence evolutionists gain no great simplicity or parsimony. True, creationists cannot identify created Genesis kinds (or bara-mins: *bara*—"created"; *min*—"kind"), but *all* the fossil, plant, and animal breeding records can be used to support conclusively that *real gaps* have existed, and continue to exist, between 46 different kinds of organisms, i.e., *fixity of kinds.*

Explanations and Simplicity

Modern Creationism			Empirical Facts	Modern Evolutionism

Modern Creationism

Dog Variants   Horse Variants   Human Variants

Created Animal Kinds

AND

Moss Variants   Fern Variants   Rose Variants

Created Plant Kinds

Empirical Facts

Fossil Record —major gaps

Animal Breeding Tests —major gaps

Plant Breeding Tests —major tests

Modern Evolutionism

Mammals   Ans   Gy   M

DNA Errors

DNA Errors

F   F   F

DNA Errors   DNA Errors

Ar   Ara   Lr   In   My   M

Br   Ech   Pl   N

DNA Errors

Pr

Sp   Co

Spontaneous Generation of Life ??

A Table of Comparisons

When evolutionists stress similarities between the ape (and/or chimpanzee) and human beings in language and tool-using experiments, they usually fail to take into account known differences. Furthermore, regarding the comparison of human beings to so-called pre-historic men, evolutionists fail to denote that many, many features (including conjectured behavior) are not subject to fossilization.

Therefore the modified chart on the next page is provided to point out some important differences between the ape and modern man. (See further: Mortimer J. Adler, *The Difference of Man and the Difference It Makes* [New York: Holt, Rinehart and Winston, 1967].)

A Table of Comparisons

MODERN MAN	APES
1. Large vaulted cranium	Flattened cranium
2. Mastoid process prominent	Mastoid process absent or inconspicuous
3. Dental arch parabolic	Dental arch U-shaped
4. Canines project little, if at all	Projecting canines
5. No diastema in upper jaw	Diastema present
6. No simian shelf	Simian shelf
* 7. Lips prominent	Lips extremely thin
8. Vertebral column in 3 curves	Vertebral column in 2 curves
9. Short neural spines on cervical vertebrae	Long neural spines on cervical vertebrae
10. Relatively short arms	Relatively long arms
*11. Lower placed nipple	Higher placed nipple
*12. Female with prominent breasts	Female with flattened breasts
*13. Body relatively hairless	Body relatively hairy
*14. Body hair, when present, most prominent on ventral body surface	Body hair always present, most prominent on dorsal surface
15. No baculum *(os penis)*	Baculum present *(os penis)*
16. Deep, bowl-shaped pelvis	Shallow, flattened pelvis
*17. Bulging gluteus maximus (buttocks)	Flattened gluteus maximus
18. Linea aspara present on femur	Linea aspara absent
19. Feet different from hands	Feet similar to hands
20. Vertebral column attached more or less at center of skull base	Vertebral column attached much toward dorsal portion of skull base

Asterisk (*) indicates fleshy aspects which are not subject to fossilization. Of course, no record of behavior patterns nor physiology is available through study of the fossil record.

Impact of Modern Evolutionary Thought

In chapter 1 we helped the reader understand different consequences of belief in evolution and belief in creation. These consequences are complex for evolutionary thinking pervades and dominates *all major areas* of man's intellectual endeavors. Because complete discussion is beyond the scope of this book, the diagram on the next page is provided. Dr. Moore has completed extensive research in support of positive affirmation of the antecedents of this tremendously complicated material implication. References are provided in association with discussion of the impact of modern evolutionary thought in his articles, "Neo-Darwinism and Society" and "Should Evolution Be Taught?"

Impact of Modern Evolutionary Thought

IF research in the history of ideas can substantiate that the position of

1. Marx and Keynes in economics and social studies,
2. Freud in psychology and psychiatry,
3. Dewey in modern education,
4. Fosdick and "higher" biblical critics in modern theology,
5. Nietzsche, James, and Positivists in modern philosophy,
6. Beard in American history,
7. Frankfurter in modern jurisprudence,
8. London and Shaw in modern novels,
9. Camus, Sartre, and Heidegger in existential thought,
10. White in sociology,
11. Simpson and Dobzhansky in paleontology and modern genetics,
12. Huxley and P. Teilhard de Chardin in evolutionary humanism,

depends upon Darwinism, neo-Darwinism and/or Modern Synthetic Evolutionary World View,

Then selected indoctrination has been, and is, the lot of many modern intelligentsia, since circa 1860 to the present.

Positive affirmation of each of the antecedents in the above complex material implication is gained through full examination of the history of ideas.

Therefore, modern secular educational content results in selected indoctrination of many of the intelligentsia of the United States, and of Western Civilization, in general.

Theses on Creation/Evolution

As a final effort to bring "closure" on this complicated subject, Dr. Moore has formulated the following "Theses on Creation/ Evolution" to provide a type of Gestalt organization for the whole scope of this book.

These theses constitute generalizations gleaned from many years of extensive studies of scientists' ideas about organic evolution, natural selection, and other related topics. He has utilized hundreds of references which he now has computerized in order to prepare bibliographic reference material for other researchers. He plans also to prepare an anthology of written works by scientists who have been critical of Darwin's ideas first published in *The Origin of Species* in 1859. Such statements from books, journal articles, and essays contain thorough treatment of weaknesses and deficiencies of organic evolution, natural selection, and other related topics which have been published in *every decade* since 1859.

Introductory:

1. Alert laymen and open-minded scientists may "instruct" those who oppose the unchanging answers in the Holy Bible to questions about origins, in accordance with the following generalizations.
2. At the very center of precise scientific activity is observation plus repeated observation.
3. Thus scientific activity may be categorized into observational, descriptive, experimentally oriented work (i.e., empirical) upon which postulational, conceptual thinking (i.e., theoretical) is built, and which may be used in turn to generate further empirical activity.
4. Properly, *scientific* theoretical thinking specifically involves prior observations about particular objects and/or events plus predictions that are testable directly or indirectly by repeatable experience.
5. All time may be conveniently thought of in terms of cosmic past, cosmic present, or cosmic future.
6. Regarding true scientific considerations, the term *historical* necessarily refers *only* to the cosmic present wherein human beings may observe and experience objects and/or events.

7. Differences between observation (or experience) and theoretical formulations are basic to contradictions which modern scientists meet in a variety of means.
8. Development of concepts of scientists may be closely coordinated with tools of scientists.

RE: Origin of Universe:
9. Attention must be called regularly to the empirical nature of cosmology and the highly imaginative nature of cosmogony.
10. Description of stellar objects and studies of relational motions of stellar objects generally comprise the science of the cosmos (cosmology).
11. Conceptual formulations of "big bang" expansion and/or steady state existence of components of the universe comprise examples of nonscientific speculative (imaginative cosmogonal) thinking outside the scope of aforementioned empirical *and* theoretical activities of proper *scientific* work.
12. Conceptual formulations about a world that was, a world that is, and a new heaven and new earth comprise nonscientific cosmogonal thinking, as found in 2 Peter 3.
13. Conceptual formulations about the sudden coming into existence of the universe, life, and humankind by acts of the Creator God comprise nonscientific cosmogonal thinking, according to Genesis 1—2 (representative of the Israelite, Hebrew tradition, which antedates *all* formulations in the Koran or other such sources of ideas on origins).
14. Ever since effective establishment of scientific professional activities, some men have directed their thoughts in absolutistic patterns of dogmas, or -isms, disregarding the identifiable properly limiting principles of scientific activities. (N.B. Empiricism, Naturalism, Evolutionism)

RE: Origin of Life:
15. Life is known *only* in complex organization, though admittedly in single-cell (as well as multiple-cell) patterns, but never in simple form.
16. All conceptualization about appearance of the first life on the earth (macrozoic, microzoic, submicrozoic, cosmozoic, and theozoic) are *nonscientific*.

129

17. All efforts directed at production of living material in the laboratory utilize already existing materials, and thus creation is *not* involved; rather, synthesis is involved.
18. Supposed spontaneous generation of life at sub-microscopic level inherently involves exclusion of all external intervention, and hence spontaneous generation can never be simulated in the laboratory.
19. DNA configurations of elements are all of "left-handed" organization in living organisms.
20. Accidental change (i.e., mutations) of DNA configurations are never known to be sources of new physical traits in living things.
21. DNA configurations are the "code" for development of physical characteristics in animals, plants, and human beings, but no "code of the code" or design for appearance of the DNA code is known.

RE: Origin of Humankind:
22. The "explanation" of origin of three kinds of rocks (igneous, sedimentary, and metamorphic) is an imaginative conceptualization primarily.
23. The geologic column, as a unit, is not based on observation and thus any derived age of the earth from the "constructed" geologic column is *only* man's deduced estimation.
24. Imagined broad degree of change of living (and fossilized) things involving supposed change of kind from common ancestral kind (i.e., *across* kind) through other common ancestry is megaevolution.
25. No absolute ages of rocks, but only ratios of elements, are derived from radiometric dating methods, which are deficient in many respects.
26. Limited degree of change of empirically documented changes *within* kind is essentially genetic variation within limits (and sometimes called micro-evolution, though the term is quite unnecessary).
27. Evidence derived by scientific activities may be classified in two main categories: circumstantial (that evidence which is basis of more than one conclusion) and conclusive (that evidence which is basis of only one conclusion).
28. There are essentially seven major categories of scientific

130

data used by proponents of models of origin: genetic variation, classification, comparative form or anatomy, comparative embryos, geographic distribution, fossil evidences, and
dating estimates.

29. A proponent of the uniformitarian evolution model of origin
bases his presumption of common ancestry by organic evolution (magaevolution) upon circumstances of similarities between and among organisms (living and fossilized) that he
detects in seven major categories of scientific data.

30. A proponent of the catastrophic creation model of origin
bases his declaration about the conclusive distinctness of
organism groups upon points of separateness and differences
between organisms (living and fossilized) that he detects in
seven major categories of scientific data (i.e., the exact same
data used by proponents of the opposing model of origins).

31. The specifically important assumption upon which the entire
imaginary, supposed megaevolutionary changes of the proponent of the uniformitarian evolution model of origin rests is:
the degree of relationship depends upon (or is a function of)
the degree of similarity.

32. "Living Fossils" constitute an excellent empirical basis for
maintaining objectively the concept of fixity of kinds.

33. Oil and coal production, as a result of methods of modern
technologists, constitute adequate empirical basis to challenge the concept of a very, very old earth (i.e., the earth
may be very young).

34. Polystrate tree trunk fossils, multiple mass burials, exposure of sedimentary rock layers all around the world, and
dinosaur tracks and human-like tracks circumstantially sit-
uated *in the same rock layers,* plus other multiple sets of
data, are bases for catastrophic changes of the earth's surface.

35. Specifically, ubiquitously evident, exposed sedimentary formations all over the earth are adequate circumstantial bases
in the rocks of a world-wide flood (i.e., the Noachian Flood).

36. Concepts of so-called human "evolution" and inclusion of
the concept of "evolutionary" origin in every major discipline of man's knowledge are explicit examples of multiple
impact of the totally unscientific uniformitarian evolution
model of origin.

Other Books Available From
Creation-Life Publishers
P. O. Box 15666
San Diego, California 92115

Manipulating Life: Where Does It Stop?
Duane T. Gish and Clifford Wilson
Two top scientists and educators discuss the ethical and moral aspects of biological engineering, cloning, test-tube babies, surrogate motherhood, abortion, recombinant DNA, and genetic manipulation. Can man "control his own evolution?" Can he create supermen—or superclones . . . or will he ultimately create monsters?

No. 100, Cloth

Causes and Cure of the Drug Epidemic
A. E. Wilder-Smith
Top scientist in Europe and the United States, formerly in charge of the drug abuse program for the NATO forces, addresses one of the top problems in this nation today. This book discusses the "drug culture"; pharmacological considerations operating in drug abuse; drug dependence and withdrawal; tranquilizers and our mechanized society; trips, flash backs, and hallucinations.

No. 032, Paper

Creation-Evolution—The Controversy
R. L. Wysong
This is a book of daring adventure between two emotionally charged spheres of thought. All who profess a love of knowledge and seek to advance science will find Dr. Wysong's treatment worthy of more than the usual attention. His probings and the fascinating array of 138 illustrations, make this book a reservoir of information that will not draw dust on your bookshelf.

No. 040, Paper

The Natural Sciences Know Nothing of Evolution
A. E. Wilder-Smith
Examines the evidence and presents the conclusions in a comprehensive analysis of evolution from the viewpoint of the Natural Sciences. Recommended for teachers and college students, as well as laymen with a special interest in the study of origins.　　**No. 110, Paper**

Children's Travel Guide & Activities Book
Jim & Darline Robinson
A book of fascinating activities to occupy the minds of children of varying ages . . . whether you are actually taking the trip described, or just visiting these exciting places by way of your imagination. Games, puzzles, and Scripture exercises with a specific aim . . . revealing the God of creation in all the wondrous sights you can explore. This first book—others to come—takes you to Colorado, Utah, and New Mexico. Also contains helpful information about facilities at various recreation spots, etc. If you plan to visit our evolution-oriented national parks, you will want to instruct your children prior to your arrival about the scientifically accurate alternative to the story they will hear about the origin of these locations. This book is an excellent and enjoyable way to do just that. 8½" x 11".　　**No. 033, Paper**

Dinosaur ABC's
Lowest level in the popular Origins: Two-Model series. Captivating illustrations; two color throughout. This book for 4-6 year olds teaches the ABC's using dinosaurs and other words related to origins at a reading level even the very young can comprehend. 8½" x 11".
No. 048, Paper; No. 049, Cloth
Teacher's Guide No. 514, Paper

Creation of Life
A. E. Wilder-Smith
Evaluates the practicing evolutionist's experimental design and data. Points out that scientific materialism hold the key to *neither* man's origin *nor* his destiny. Emphasizes that in order to have an efficient *design,* you must first have an efficient *designer.*　　**No. 039, Paper**

Tracking Those Incredible Dinosaurs . . . And The People Who Knew Them

John D. Morris

What's the *real* story on those footprints in the Paluxy River bed? What do they really tell us? An eye-witness report documented by nearly 200 photographs. Dr. Morris, highly qualified in geoscience, examines the historical evidence, as well as the existing evidence found in a near-by river of the small Texas town of Glen Rose, which has recently become the center of much controversy. Did man and dinosaurs live together in ancient times? *Look at these photos and draw your own conclusions.*

No. 173, Paper

He Who Thinks Has To Believe

A. E. Wilder-Smith

Explores the marvelous process of reasoning and drawing logical conclusions, with the result that anyone who uses these natural abilities of the mind properly, *must* arrive at the conclusion that there is a Creator-God.

No. 077, Paper

Decade of Creation

Fourth in the popular series of collections of "Impact Articles" and reports of action on the "front-lines" of the battle to regain an equal place for scientific creationism. These articles originally appeared in ICR's *Acts & Facts* 1978 and 1979.   **No. 044, Paper**

Scientific Creationism

Henry M. Morris, Ph.D.

Most comprehensive, documented exposition of all the scientific evidence of origins. Scientific data presented without bias, followed (in the general edition only) by an extensive discussion of the biblical aspects of creationism.

General Edition (biblical documentation)   **No. 140, Paper**
Public School Edition (non-religious text)   **No. 141, Paper;**
                                             No. 357, Cloth

Evolution? The Fossils Say NO!

Duane T. Gish, Ph.D.

The only *solid* evidence in the discussion of origins is the fossil record—anything else is circumstantial evidence and conjecture. Powerful testimony about the origin of our earth's inhabitants. Over 100,000 in print.

General Edition **No. 054, Paper**
Public School Edition (non-religious text) **No. 055, Paper**

The Troubled Waters of Evolution

Henry M. Morris, Ph.D.

In addition to presenting a nontechnical study of the evidencce for creation, this book traces the history of evolutionary thought and specifies the areas of our society that have been devastated by it. **No. 170, Paper**

The Genesis Flood

Henry M. Morris, Ph.D., and John C. Whitcomb, Th.D.

Comprehensive scientific exposition of creation and the Flood, with pertinent data supporting the creation/catastrophism position. Widely recognized as the most authoritative book on this subject. In its 25th printing.

No. 069, Paper

Many Infallible Proofs

Henry M. Morris, Ph.D.

Scripturally and logically supports each basic tenet of the Christian faith. A real help to personal growth and effective witnessing in today's skeptical society. Used as a college textbook in Apologetic and Christian Evidence courses.

No. 102, Kivar; No. 103, Cloth

The Genesis Record

Henry M. Morris, Ph.D.

A one-of-a-kind scientific and devotional commentary on the book of beginnings. Both theologians and lay persons will gain great understanding of this foundational book of the Bible. **No. 070, Cloth**

The Bible Has The Answer
Henry M. Morris, Ph.D., and Martin Clark, D.Ed.
Biblical and reasonable answers to 150 of the most frequently asked—and perplexing—questions about the Christian faith and daily life. **No. 023, Paper**

Why Does God Allow It?
A. E. Wilder-Smith, Ph.D.
If there is a God—who is supposed to be "good" and loving—why does He permit all the violence and suffering in the world? Does the abundance of evil prove He really doesn't exist? Sensible answers to questions that have plagued people since the beginning. Gripping photos
No. 186, Paper

Dinosaurs: Those Terrible Lizards
Duane T. Gish, Ph.D.
Did dinosaurs and humans live at the same time? Are dragons just imaginary? This beautifully color-illustrated book for children tells about dinosaurs and why they no longer exist. 8½" x 11". **No. 046, Cloth**

Dry Bones . . . and Other Fossils
Gary E. Parker, M.S., Ed.D.
What are fossils? How are they formed? What can we learn from them? Answers in conversational dialogue in this creatively illustrated book for children. 8½" x 11".
No. 047, Paper

What's In An Egg?
Joan Gleason Budai
Many things get their start in eggs. This book lays the groundwork for a truthful, open discussion when asked, "Where did I come from?" Through pictures and plain talk, *What's In An Egg?* tell the story from "egg" to actual birth. **No. 185, Paper**

Crash Go the Chariots
Clifford Wilson, Ph.D.
The "million +" bestseller rebuttal to von Daniken's imaginative speculations in *Chariots of the Gods.*
No. 035, Paper

1980's Decade of Shock
Clifford Wilson, Ph.D., and John Weldon

It's no secret that the world is in a mess. If a nuclear war doesn't kill us, the environment filled with chemical pollutants might. But then with the economy and energy hassles, who cares anyway! Fortunately, God is still in control, and we can discover the spiritual implications and eternal significance of our chaotic, confusing, frightening times in this book that offers hope for a hopeless situation. Foreword by Tim LaHaye.

No. 045, Paper

Occult Shock and Psychic Forces
Clifford Wilson, Ph.D., and John Weldon

The relatively obvious occult involvements have expanded to include more subtle forms of deception—parapsychology, hypnosis, est, acupuncture, and holistic medicine. This activity is rampant—you need to be aware of it. You need to read this timely book.   **No. 113, Paper**